ALSO BY MARGOT FONTEYN

Autobiography

This is a Borzoi Book
published in New York by Alfred A. Knopf.

A DANCER'S WORLD

MARGOT FONTEYN

A DANCER'S WORLD

An Introduction
for Parents and Students

ALFRED A. KNOPF   New York

1979

THIS IS A BORZOI BOOK PUBLISHED BY
ALFRED A. KNOPF, INC.

ACKNOWLEDGMENTS

I would like to express my warmest thanks to
Mrs. Patricia M. Mackenzie, B.B., A.R.A.D., and to Miss Valerie
Taylor, A.R.A.D., of the Royal Academy of Dancing, and
to Mr. Terry Westmoreland, of the Royal Ballet, for their
very helpful suggestions and comments.

—MARGOT FONTEYN

Acknowledgments for permission to reproduce photographs
and illustrations are given on pages 127–8.

Library of Congress Cataloging in Publication Data
Fonteyn, Margot, Dame, [date]   A dancer's world.
1. Dancing.   2. Ballet.   3. Dancing—Vocational guidance.
I. Title.   GV1594.F66   793.3   78–20442
ISBN 0–394–50448–8

Manufactured in the United States of America

First American Edition

To the memory of
GRACE BOSUSTOW,
my first dancing teacher

CONTENTS

THE PHOTOGRAPHS HAVE BEEN CHOSEN TO GIVE
AN IMPRESSION RATHER THAN TO ILLUSTRATE
THE SUBJECT MATTER.

INTRODUCTION

The world of dance is a charmed place. Some people like to inhabit it, others to behold it; either way it is rewarding. Those who look in from the outside are the spectators who love the beauty, the colors, the music, the drama, and the physical prowess of the dancers. The more they see, the more they enjoy the great moments of excitement in the theatre and discover the small moments of grace and the tiny vignettes of acting.

It is a world that takes hold of its observers in an unusual way, by presenting some aspects of the universal ideal with which they momentarily identify as the dancers make their kaleidoscopic patterns over the stage.

For those who live in this magic world, it has an even stronger hold. Life has an extra dimension of expression, wordless but powerful. If we limit our means of communication to the mind and head, we need to have very rare minds of the kind that contains such a wealth of resources, in knowledge and abilities, that all its energies can be deployed in thinking.

Many of us do not have such minds but the rest of our bodies help in expressing our emotions. Without counting the Italians, who have a spectacular language of the hands with which to emphasize their conversation, almost everyone makes use of gesture to accentuate a point of speech. Public speakers are among the best examples. Dancing carries the development of this physical expression to ultimate limits. It is by no means just a series of exercises and gymnastics, but an art in which no two performers are identical, because each one puts into it something of himself, his very soul.

I am not talking only of stage performances but of any kind of dancing, no matter how unpretentious. The world of dance is a natural world from which civilization has divorced many of us by making it appear remote—something reserved for the few who have a special talent. That is because we associate dancing more with theatre than with the daily round of living and religious rites in which it was originally employed. The soul then was very much involved in the dance. It is not surprising that a primitive tribesman who witnessed European social dancing late in the last century expressed his disgust with the frivolous purpose for which it was used by white people. In fact, by setting dance somewhat apart from normal life we only waste a valuable aspect of living.

There are many ways in which we can exploit the gift of dance. I have tried to suggest all the possibilities and how they can best be located. It would be impossible to list dancing academies unless one instituted a kind of *Michelin Guide*, like the one for hotels and restaurants, with quality ratings reviewed annually. I am not in favor of such a project. My purpose is rather to indicate the choices but to emphasize that the decisions are all personal, for each individual is different, each case is different. I would recommend readers to go through this book carefully, then put it down and follow their intelligence and instinct.

In addition to some guidelines on approaching

dance as a theatre art, it is hoped that the book will open doors for all those interested in uniting mind and body in the most comprehensive means of expression and communication. Lack of communication between people is one of the sources of evil in our world, so let us consider dance not as a rare vocation but as a blessing granted to all who have the inclination to enjoy it.

PART ONE

In 1977 over twenty million people bought
tickets to ballet and dance performances,
which compared with only fifteen million
who bought tickets to National Football
League games. And it's even more significant
when taken in comparison to the one million
people who attended ballet and dance
performances in 1964; it is a real explosion;
it is the most popular and fastest growing
performing-art-form in America.

—PETER ROSENWALD,
DANCE CRITIC OF *The Wall Street Journal*

DANCING

One of the best things to be said about dancing is that, like all the arts, there is really no end to it. Therefore it is always interesting, and no sooner has one learned one thing than one realizes how much more there is still to know. With each lesson a little progress only opens up more possibilities.

Of course it is easy to lose enthusiasm for a pursuit that seems too difficult. On the other hand, there is always the chance to improve and that is a great attraction; for, generally speaking, we are all happier when we are still striving for achievement than when the prize is in our hands. And, in working on the stage, even when we hold the prize it is only for a fleeting moment—a few short hours of performance and the cascade of applause at the end. But the next performance must be fought for and won all over again.

There is nothing better for children than an absorbing interest; they have such restless little minds and it keeps them out of mischief—for a while, at least. The arts are perfect for that because they are eternal. I sometimes wonder if art is not meant for children, or at least if there isn't an artist lurking in every child. Those who have more pressing abilities or vocations to develop leave the artist in them in abeyance, or even forget about it as they grow up; whereas those

3

who become artists continue always to see life with some of the fantasy of childhood, which forms a kind of protective barrier around their sensibilities.

When considering the arts for children, one can only give them all the options. Dancing, if the child should have some feeling for it, is more communal than painting or music. The pianist practices alone, and drawing and painting are individual pursuits not dependent on others. But dancers work together, always conscious of each other and often subordinating their efforts to the unity of the whole.

It is almost impossible to turn dancing into anything malevolent or really unpleasant or even mean. So the practice of dancing brings people together in a friendly spirit. How much easier it is to have an argument in words than in dance; yet two dancers at a party or a nightclub are certainly in communication even if they don't say a word to each other.

In a way, dance is a language without words; there is communication and contact among the participants through their relationships in lines, circles, or groups. Each step has its direction and pattern, making dancing a well-ordered occupation with well-defined rules. And what a relief that can sometimes be in a life so full of choices and decisions! I think children like to know exactly what is expected of them, because they are basically logical and hate a lot of uncertainty and confusion.

To the minds of most people in the modern world, dancing classes are relegated to the province of children—little girls in particular—and to a special breed of people who are professional dancers. If we look back a little in history, however, we find that dancing was an obligatory social accomplishment in the seventeenth and eighteenth centuries, and "the dancing lesson" was a necessary feature of life for all adults of the upper levels of society.

Surprisingly, the steps that those gentlemen dancing masters in satin knee breeches, lace ruffles, and powdered wigs were so busy teaching to the golden youth of Europe in their day were, oftentimes, the very same steps that thousands of little girls in pink tights, leotards, and neatly pinned hair are now learning all across the world, from China to Peru. The *chassé*, *coupé*, pirouette, and *pas de bourrée* are not inventions of a rarefied world of modern ballet, but simply the steps of that old and dignified dance of the ballroom, the minuet. So let us not think of ballet and dance as pastimes far removed from the lives of ordinary mortals. Dance has always been, and always will be, a very basic form of human expression and communication.

CHILDREN

Everyone wants to know at what age children should start dancing lessons. In fact, the choice of teacher is more important than the age of the pupil.

Full ballet training, for example, is not recommended before children are nine or ten years old, but children's classes with a responsible teacher can be started from five on. Lessons could be once a week and there would definitely be no dancing on the toes.

Ballet classes for children up to the ages of ten or twelve are something for everyone—the slender, the lumpy, the gawky, the clumsy, and the talented alike. For the last group, they are also a preparation for professional training but should be specifically designed for children—and children are not "ballerinas." The idea of an infant prodigy used to be appealing to some parents (and to some audiences), but it is definitely not encouraged in the world of professional ballet, where even the stars are basically part of a uniform group.

The world of dance is not comparable to the acting world, in which there are roles requiring actual children with appropriate voices. Most "children" in ballet are danced by adult artists, except in those companies, like the Kirov, the Royal Danish Ballet, and the New York City Ballet, where children from the associated professional school take part in *The Nut-cracker*, *Coppélia*, and so forth. But this is deliberate professional training for specially selected children. The vast majority of young children going to ballet class would learn only the basic positions and exercises, and elementary steps combined in simple little dances to be performed at the annual school recital. Without the child realizing it, this work gives a sense of physical coordination. It serves admirably for sports and games, as well as exercising the mind in an effort of concentration completely different from that required for school studies.

Ballet is by no means the only type of dance for young children, but I talk about it more fully because it is the most complex, and because the field of ballet schools is also rather complex for the parent wanting to give a child the best opportunity at the right age.

Where young children are concerned, I do not believe it is necessary or right to overemphasize the difficulties of ballet training. I mean that when I was a child, no one ever told me, "You will have to be prepared to work hard and be very dedicated if you want to become a ballerina." If someone had, I am sure it would have put me off. Luckily, my mother took me to a good teacher who made the lessons enjoyable and interesting, so my dancing thrived.

It is rather important for mothers to understand that it is not in their power to make prodigies, stars, or anything else. Their children are what they are, and no amount of ambition or determination on the parent's part will alter the facts. If the child has talent, there is no need for a "pushy" parent, and if the child has no talent, there is nothing to be done except to realize it. There is no sense in imposing a burden on the child that he or she cannot live up to.

When I was young, there was no kind of pressure

involved. If I entered an examination or a competition, or if I was to dance in a school display, there was a lot of excitement in the preparation, and I was even unconsciously nervous, but that was all part of the fun. It was interesting, but never too serious. Above everything else, I think dancing should be a happy affair. It is, after all, the most spontaneous expression of elation. "Jumping for joy" is a very basic human reaction, and a child skipping down the street is simply an untrained dancer.

EARLY TRAINING

With dancing there is no question that the single most important factor is a good teacher. It is very discouraging to find after years of training that one is doing everything wrong and, in addition, that it takes a lot more time to put it right than it would have done to learn it properly in the first place. This is because the limbs themselves have to know what to do—and they learn far more slowly than the brain. If one tries to correct a movement that has been wrongly taught, the body has to unlearn what it was doing and start all over again—a double process. This is a silly waste of time and effort. Certain elementary rules in ballet should be learned correctly from the first day. The most important concerns stance, or placement, sometimes referred to by that even more comically Victorian word "posture." It means that the child should stand up straight, head erect, spine vertical, shoulders down—no slumping, sagging, or bulging.

So far no great problem. But then comes the "turn-out." Turnout is generally thought of as turning the feet so that the toes point out to the sides instead of to the front. But it is not just the feet that must turn but the whole leg from the hip joint.

This turnout is the most difficult part of early training. Each child is constructed differently; some have loose hip joints, others have a very restricted range of movement. Teachers have to assess what is right for each child. The common fault is to turn the feet out farther than the knees and the hips, which results in what is called "rolling in." The best way to judge how far the feet can turn out to the sides is by standing with the heels touching and the feet turned out, and then bending the knees. As long as the knees are directly *above* the toes (not in front of them), it is correct—*provided* that the spine is straight and vertical. In other words, anyone can get it right by letting the bottom stick out, but that is no good.

To test the position, the whole back is held flat against a wall, with the heels almost touching the wall, too. Then, when the knees bend *above* the toes of the turned-out feet (the shoulders and back sliding gently down the wall), it is easy to judge how far the hip joint will turn naturally. If the feet are turned too far out, the knees will no longer be directly above the toes but will move forward and pull the ankles forward with them so that the feet are "rolling in."

What is wrong with "rolling in" is that the *whole* sole of the foot is no longer in firm contact with the floor, and it is that contact which is the most valuable thing a dancer has. From it come stability, control, and, most important of all, the power to spring up into the air. If, for example, an arrow is bent or crooked, it loses speed and cannot fly as it would if it were straight. Similarly, a dancer jumping in the air is like a crooked arrow if the push-off comes from a "rolled in" ankle. To make a really good arrow, of course, the knees must be very braced and straight, too.

Again, if a chair or table has one leg slightly shorter than the other, we all know it will wobble as soon as weight is put on that corner. It's rather the same for a person standing on one turned-out leg with the other raised high. If *all* the sole of the foot is evenly on the floor, the dancer will balance well, but if the foot is rolling over and most of the weight is on that forward side of the foot, he or she will be wobbly.

The important thing, therefore, even in a beginners' class, is care and attention to placement and turnout. At first the legs are turned out as far as they can go naturally without the danger of feet rolling in, and very gradually, as a little strength is developed in the muscles, the legs are turned a bit farther from the hips; however, some children will never have a good turnout; their physical construction will not permit it. It is dangerous to *force* even the more supple ones, because their bones are growing and still soft.

The question of when a student should first have toeshoes is one on which it is better to be safe than sorry. The answer is: not before the feet are prepared to take the strain, which might be after about three years of serious training.

Some types of physique are more vulnerable to strain in early training than others, and a good teacher these days is expected to have an adequate knowledge of anatomy. One cannot be too careful with young children. Do not be misled by pictures of Russian children standing strongly on their toes with straight legs and tightly braced knees at the age of ten. Those are the ones specially selected from among thousands and subjected to rigorous physical examination. Even so, there is a difference of opinion about the necessity of acquiring so much mastery so young. In the School of American Ballet, toe work is not taught before two or three years of preparation.

From all this, one can see just how advisable it is to go to a good teacher in the first place. "If a thing is worth doing, it is worth doing well," my grandmother used to say, and to my mind they are words of eternal truth.

TEACHERS

You may well ask, "How do I find a good teacher?" To this there is no very easy answer.

Of course, if you live in a small town you may not have a choice; you must trust to luck with your only local dancing school. Nevertheless, you can make some useful observations and do a bit of research.

Apart from my explanations of placement and turnout, which might be a bit difficult to understand at first, there are some general observations you can make, which, when all added together, will help in the assessment of your teacher, such as:

- Does she have authority and assurance when teaching?
- Does she insist on pupils being neatly dressed (and is she neatly dressed herself)?
- Does she hold the attention of the class, or are the younger ones running about chattering and out of control?
- Does she generally give a lot of corrections or just show the steps and let the pupils get on as best they can?
- Does she try to vary the lesson sometimes, or does she mechanically repeat the same exercises at each class?

- Does she demonstrate the movements carefully and take trouble over getting them right, or does she seem to think that limbering and high kicks are all that matter?
- Does she have some good common sense?

Without being either overdramatic or plain boring, a teacher should somehow manage to get the serious concentration of her pupils. They will then respond with that bit of extra effort to get something right, and she should follow it with a word of encouragement when they are successful.

A teacher who continually gives little individual corrections inspires more attention from her pupils than the one who only addresses the whole class occasionally with a blanket comment. One who gives almost no corrections at all is not giving true value—although it is fair to remember that a big class of young beginners is almost too much for one person to handle. Some teachers use the assistance of senior students to correct the tiny children so that each one gets some individual help.

I have tried earlier to explain exactly what is meant by technical terms like "turnout" and "rolling in" because technique provides the foundation on which the ballet dancer's final accomplishment is built—just as a house must have a solid basis of support or it will always be insecure. But the kind of house that is built on that foundation is quite another matter, open to endless possibilities. It could be purely functional, lacking in style or even ugly; it could be charming to look at, having graceful lines; it could be an efficient building but without any special interest; it could be a noble and beautiful mansion of perfect proportions; or it could have some special individual features of its own.

And so also with the dancer: what matters is what is built on the foundation. The technique is only there to allow the fullest control and the fullest range of movement, but the movement alone is not enough; it is merely exercise—the efficient house of no special interest. From that point, the artist—or architect—goes forward into personal expression in the creation of his art. With a developed technique, the dancer is able to express emotional and dramatic situations or pure grace and beauty in movement.

It may seem premature to look so far ahead when talking of teachers for young children, but every good teacher has an innate sense of what dance really means. She does not teach it in any precise way; she imparts it because it is somewhere in her own movements as she demonstrates to the children. They absorb it as children absorb everything the teacher has to give them.

Generally speaking, I do not think it is too difficult to recognize a good teacher when you find one; but it would be wise to look around and be sure you have the best that is available.

The dance magazines offer a lot of information by way of advertisements and reports on various schools but, of course, it is only information and requires a certain amount of deduction to distinguish between the good and the merely adequate. In the end, trial and error might be the best way to decide between two or three alternatives.

I think most teachers these days attend conference weeks or various refresher courses held by the dance teachers' organizations of different countries. After all, no one teaches badly except out of ignorance, and we all know that there is never any end to learning.

LOCAL DANCE
SCHOOLS

Local dancing schools vary enormously in the types of dance they offer. Broadly speaking, the schools fall into three groups. One would specialize in "show dancing," as required for musicals and commercial theatre, TV and films, and so on, which includes jazz, tap, and modern dance. Many such schools now offer ballet classes as well, because so many basically ballet-trained dancers work in the field of stage dancing.

However, a student hoping to find a place in a ballet company would look for the type of school that definitely specializes in ballet. Such a school might also teach modern dance, and possibly Spanish or other national or ethnic dances.

The third group is that of schools specializing in modern dance on the highest level. They do not normally offer a variety of other styles. The directors of these schools have been trained in one of the well-known systems of modern dance, such as Martha Graham's or Lester Horton's. The technique is very different from ballet and must be studied just as seriously.

Many of the specialist ballet schools are directed by professional dancers of high standing, whose long experience on the stage gives them unique knowledge. Such teachers have their own individual contribution to give their pupils. It is based on their personal attributes as performers, and each one is different. It is in this very personal way that the art of ballet has been handed down from generation to generation for three hundred years. The older artists help to develop the young, not just in the exercises and technique but in their presentation on stage. The steps learned in school are merely the alphabet of movement; when they are linked together in a ballet, there are a thousand different ways in which they can be made significant, just as words or phrases can be made clumsy or poetic according to the way they are spoken. It is the ability to convey these nuances that makes a true artist.

There are also many first-rate teachers who have not been great dancers on the stage. They often understand and inspire the younger children and perhaps have more patience with them. Teaching is a different talent from that of performing; the two do not necessarily go together in the same person. Each teacher should be taken finally on his or her own merits, and in relation to the point of development the student has reached.

Studio premises can present problems for the local ballet teacher. In many cities it is difficult, or prohibitively expensive, to find suitably spacious accommodation and equip it with the right flooring, *barres*,* and mirrors. For small children, some compromise arrangement is adequate, but it is never desirable to use the back of a chair for support instead of a properly secured rail, and serious students do require a traditional studio. It need not be enormous but should

---

* *Barres* are rails that the students hold on to for support during the first part of the class; they are fixed to the wall or to movable stands at about elbow height.

have a non-slippery floor surface, either wood or lino-leum, which ideally should not be laid directly on concrete, as that is bad for the muscles. The *barres* should be fixed to the walls, or if portable, well steadied by weights. Mirrors are a necessity for the older students.

Last, a word about music. A surprising number of dancers are quite unmusical—and some teachers, too—partly because so much attention has to go into doing the steps that little is left over to concentrate on fitting them to the music. There was a time when it would have been unthinkable to have a dance class without a pianist, but the economics of small private businesses today make a pianist a luxury at least, sometimes an impossibility.

It is a sad fact that many teachers are forced to used taped music. No matter how fine the recording, there remains something impersonal about it, and it makes fewer demands upon the student to use his or her ears.

It is hard to advise on the type of dance school to aim for; I think ballet is the safest first choice when there is doubt, because it is easier to go from ballet into show dancing or modern than the reverse. Also the quality of show dancing is considerably higher, and its artistic value greater, now that ballet is so popular and has had much influence on stage dancing.

If you are choosing a show-dancing school, look for the same happy atmosphere that is desirable in all dance classes. A will to work on the part of the children is good, and the competitive spirit is fine, too, but not when it takes the joy out of dance.

Dance is essentially an art that gives health and happiness, and it should not be allowed to breed evil jealousies, bad character, or nervous breakdowns. The old stories of rivals—either the dancers or their mothers—slashing costumes and putting ground glass in each other's shoes before the show might be true, for all I know, but they have nothing to do with art. And art is the most satisfying element in any type of dancing, whether in sparkling musicals, grand ballets, or significant modern innovations.

The majority of local dance schools hold special classes for adult beginners in ballet, modern, jazz, tap, or Spanish dance—classes that are immensely popular, even with people well into middle age.

EXAMINATIONS

While we are on the subject of the independent local schools, it is worth noting that there are one or two important dance organizations that hold examinations—principally in ballet—in many parts of the world. The exams are open to pupils of any school that will prepare them in the set syllabus and enter sufficient candidates to make the examiner's visit worthwhile. They approximate roughly to examinations in music.

The point of these examinations is twofold. First, they really examine the teachers—because a pupil's performance is the result of the teacher's ability. A pupil with bad faults is the product of an ignorant teacher. Second, the examinations assess the abilities of the child or student in relation to others of his or her approximate age group elsewhere, perhaps in larger cities or even other countries.

The examinations serve as a yardstick for pupils, parents, and teachers to measure how the students stand generally in the whole field of dance training, and in this context have an unarguable value. However, it has to be understood that they are only a test: the exams do not make the dancers; they only assess, and the certificates are not passports to employment. No one engages a dancer purely on the basis of his or

her credits on paper. To get a job, the dancer must be seen dancing, and each ballet company tends toward a preference for a particular type of dancer.

These examinations are usually divided into two groups: for young children and for teen-age students. The examinations for small children are very short —ten to twenty minutes—and for advanced students an hour, at least. The systems of marking and the certificates vary with each organization; also the syllabuses and markings are updated from time to time as considered necessary.

One should know that the markings in the children's group of exams are not, and certainly should not be, set to any "professional" standard. That is to say that a high result for a girl of ten or twelve, for example, would not necessarily indicate that you have a future ballerina on your hands; although in rare cases you just might. It would mean, however, that she is above average and you would be justified in moving her on to serious training. The difference between a child with good examination results and a serious student is about the same as that between a big fish in a small pool and a little sprat in the ocean. There is never any harm in trying to make the transition, but it is a good idea to keep an open mind and not to expect too much.

In America several different groups hold annual examinations; one such is Britain's Royal Academy of Dancing, which examines about three thousand students every year. In addition, there are also the Cecchetti Council of America, the Imperial Society of Teachers of Dancing, as well as various other dance-teacher organizations.

BALLET AND
GENERAL EDUCATION

Apart from the specialist local ballet schools, there are performing arts schools that give a full general education as well as full ballet training. The reason for combined schools is obvious: it is so much easier to fit dancing into the schedule of general education if both take place in the same school. Economically it is not so easy, because it requires a double staff. The arrangement varies according to the subsidy—if any—that is available. For example, students of the Russian theatre schools, which are entirely state-supported, can be resident with full academic tuition from their acceptance until graduation eight years later. After graduation they are expected to make their careers wherever they are directed—in ballet companies or possibly folk dance companies.

In most European opera houses, which are also state-subsidized, the pupils attend the theatre school for general education and ballet but live at home.

The Royal Ballet School in London—partially state-subsidized—has a resident junior school, and a nonresident senior school to complete the dance training after school-leaving age. The School of American Ballet in New York is part-subsidized, nonresident, and not general educational, but gives a full ballet training up to graduation.

All these schools are attached to ballet companies, and the best graduates are taken into the companies whenever there are vacancies. The pupils' training in the school gives them a necessary unity of style.

There are also a few combined schools run on a regular commercial basis in England and the United States, and some in Europe.

The normal age for entry in a professional school is nine or ten years. Even at that age, a child with bad faults might find them hard to eradicate. In such circumstances, the school would give preference to a child with no previous training at all. Failure to be accepted by the school can cause a big crisis of discouragement; yet the child is only ten! The selection has been made mainly on physical suitability, and although other children may have better backs, legs, and feet, they may have less real feeling for dance, which is a more nebulous quality. Perhaps a talent occasionally slips through the net.

An alternative system, which seems to work well, is that of the Australian Ballet School (attached to the Australian Ballet company), which is a high school only. In that country, where there are excellent local ballet teachers in every state, the selection for the professional school comes at fifteen or sixteen, and some very fine dancers have graduated from the school. The secret lies in the quality of teaching that the students can get before they enter the school attached to a ballet company. I believe that the local ballet schools have certain advantages but they also have a tremendous responsibility, and their teachers need to be very intelligent and enlightened to meet the challenge. That they are able to do so has been proved beyond doubt in Australia and by some excellent teachers in various countries.

BOYS

For boys it is strongly advisable to enter a school of ballet as young as possible, because they need the early training. Wherever there are opportunities for boys to get good daily ballet lessons from the age of ten or twelve years, there are superb male dancers. No longer are they the sole prerogative of Russia and Denmark; many other countries are now in the field and have produced international stars.

When I say that boys need the early training, it might sound as though it were more necessary for them than for girls. In fact, both are put at a disadvantage for professional ballet if they start too late. It is not a question, as in gymnastics, of having to start in extreme youth, but—if one discounts the once-a-week children's classes, which serve as a preparation only—eight to ten is a good age to start ballet, twelve is still all right, and after that each year is more disadvantageous than the preceding.

Training is more difficult for boys than for girls because their muscles and tendons are stronger and harder; the sooner they start the long labor of learning to move in certain patterns the better, for every bit of training facilitates coordination by making the muscles more responsive. To respond quickly, they must be familiar with the movements required of

them and in condition to perform them instantly; the tendons, too, must be as supple as possible to avoid any chance that a sudden movement will cause overstrain.

A fully professional dancer performing several times a week and training daily will feel his muscles so finely in tune that even one day off—a free Sunday —leaves him feeling that he has not practiced for a week. After forty minutes or so of exercise, his control returns and he is back in top form. A week without any dancing means another week before he is back at his peak, and a month must be paid for with a month of retraining.

A young man whose physique is fully developed and whose bones are already adult when he starts his training has to work with much less amenable material than a boy, say, twelve years old, who is still in the process of formation.

Traditionally, male dancers are divided into three types according to their physique. First, the *danseur noble*, who has elegant proportions, long legs, and a noble bearing. He dances principal roles and is expected to have control in slow movements that display the harmony of his line; he never makes a jerky movement or assumes an ugly position but dances all the steps with grace and ease, even the most difficult pirouettes and leaps.

The second type is the *demi-caractère* dancer, a little more compact in physique than the *danseur noble*, and his dances are quicker in order to show off his brilliant footwork, bounding jumps, and fast turns.

The third type was originally called *comique*—or even *grotesque*—when the ballets were mostly about mythological subjects including various fantastic creatures or beasts. These dancers are now called character dancers. They are of stocky build, never very tall, and they do all kinds of national dances and character or comic parts.

The finest male dancers move with the power and control of a tiger; they can spring into the air, twist and turn their bodies and limbs, and land gently with absolute precision. There is no visible trace of the effort involved. Men who rise to fame in the dance world are like a small aristocracy. Although actors can be counted in thousands, male dancers are only reckoned in hundreds, and the finest among them number less than a dozen.

Dance definitely holds as much scope for men as for women—probably more so. The history of ballet was started by dancing masters who established the first principles and wrote the first books on technique. For a short period when men dropped almost completely out of ballet, it very nearly died. Luckily they are now securely back again and occupy a highly honored position in the art.

BALLET SHOES

Ballet shoes have no right or left feet. When they are new, they are interchangeable until the dancer works them in and decides which goes better on which foot. They should more accurately be called slippers, as they are derived from the light silk slippers worn by fashionable ladies to evening dances in the last century. The French still call them *chaussons*, meaning slippers, rather than *chaussures*, meaning shoes.

There are soft ballet shoes and blocked, or point, shoes (toeshoes). The soft shoes are worn by boys and men. They are made in canvas or in very light leather lined with canvas. The undersole is much smaller than the sole of the foot, so that the dancer's toes and part of his heel stand on the soft upper leather, which is turned back under the foot and pleated into the sole underneath the toes. The soles should be thin and very flexible so that the dancer can arch his instep and stretch his toes unimpeded by the shoe.

Girls wear the same soft shoes in either canvas or leather when they begin to learn simple children's dancing or ballet, and, later on, in certain roles that do not require toe work. If the shoes are too rigid, the foot muscles cannot exercise properly and do not develop strength. The shoes should be flexible. In fact, they are best when they are old and have become as pliant as a glove.

Point shoes (from *sur la pointe* in French, meaning "on the point," or standing on the points of the toes) are also called toeshoes. They are made of satin and have a reinforced sole that gives support to the lower arch of the foot when standing on point, and the toe of the shoe is strengthened with an extra layer of canvas hardened with paste. The point of the shoe is squared off so that there is a little flat area to balance on.

Ideally the shoes should be rather weak and the feet strong, but this situation is generally reversed for reasons of economy. Students cannot afford many shoes, so they want a lot of wear from each pair; consequently the shoes are overblocked and the soles—or backs—are almost rigid. As this prevents the foot muscles from exercising properly, the shoes do most of the work.

Professional dancers are accustomed to breaking their shoes down by any means, even hitting them with a hammer, until they reach a comfortable degree of pliancy.

Point shoes for use on the stage traditionally come in pink satin and are dyed to other colors by the wearer when so required. White satin—or even black —is sometimes available or can be specially ordered. The men's shoes are normally white, black, or gray.

All ballet shoes have a little drawstring that is tied at the center front and the ends tucked inside. A piece of narrow elastic should be stitched across the upper instep to hold the soft shoes on while dancing.

Point shoes have ribbons (one yard or one meter per shoe) that are crossed first in front of the ankle, then again at the back, then once more in the front and finally tied just behind the inside anklebone, with the ends tucked away from sight. They are never tied in a bow.

Elastics are often given away free when buying ballet shoes, but ribbons must usually be purchased separately. In either case, their exact placement is a matter of personal preference, and so they must be stitched on by the dancer—or by the dancer's mother!

THE MOTHER

The greatest assets one can possibly have in life are wise parents, and I was blessed with ones who made sacrifices to give me every opportunity yet always allowed me to feel that it was my career, not theirs.

"Ballet mother" was a term of dread to me when I was in my teens because certain other mothers had given all of them a dubious name. Happily, mine never gave me a moment of embarrassment: she suffered my nerves worked off onto her as though she were a cushion; she always had a meal ready when I got home from long rehearsals; she stood by me with her sense of pride well under control and out of sight. What more could one ask?

RECOLLECTIONS OF A DANCER'S MOTHER

My daughter was born on May 18, 1919. We christened her Margaret; she is now called Margot Fonteyn.

We lived in London when I took her to her first ballet class. She was not yet five years old, and I did so with no particular view to her becoming a professional dancer. Her father in fact suggested that the classes would be good for her deportment, which to me seemed an extraordinary word to use, because although when she was concentrating on a game or trying to read she would hunch her shoulders and screw up her eyes, her body was as straight as a young sapling and beautifully proportioned.

It was luck that the teacher we found, Miss Grace Bosustow, who lived around the corner from us, had the letters "A.O.D." after her name on a plate beside her gate—although I had no idea what the letters meant at the time. When we went for an interview, I noticed that the front sitting room was slightly bigger than ours and had no furniture but a piano and a few small chairs. One wall had a large mirror, and the others had wooden poles attached to them about three feet from the floor. On one of those walls was a framed picture of a certificate awarded to Grace Bosustow by the Association of Operatic Dancing (now the Royal Academy of Dancing), which of course accounted for the letters after her name. This, to me, proved that she was a qualified teacher, and that Margot would be correctly trained, although I had no idea how important this would be in later years. As for me, I had absolutely no knowledge of classical ballet. I only knew that I loved dancing and that I admired grace and fluidity of movement.

Miss Bosustow was a charming woman, and we agreed that Margot should attend the classes for juniors every Friday afternoon. Margot loved them from the start and took it all very seriously, doing her best to do exactly what she was told. She first learned the five positions of the feet and then to point her foot in front of her with the little toe on the floor.

Margot was a quick learner, a calm and determined student—qualities that are extremely important in a dancer, I believe. Miss Bosustow once wrote about Margot, "From the first I thought she was a sweet little girl and very original. Though I don't think she was shy in the usual sense of the word, she seldom spoke unless spoken to, and would never say 'yes' if a nod would do as well. Her manner was very grave and somehow remote. She was not at all vivacious, and everything she did was placid and determined."

From my point of view, in the dancing class she always looked better than the other children, moved better. Prejudice perhaps, but watching her against the others in later classes, she just looked different doing exactly the same movements. I always went along with Margot to her classes and watched—and learned. In fact, we both learned together, so that I also knew what each movement should be. This knowledge proved valuable, for when my husband's business called us abroad and we had to find new teachers, I was able to recognize a good teacher from a bad one —and that is the best thing a parent can learn. I continued to watch for the next ten years.

The great snag these days is that most teachers do not allow parents to watch their children in class. They might get invited once a month, if they are lucky. Of course, many parents can be perfect nuisances. They become jealous, ambitious, and overprotective. The trouble is that a group of mothers with children all think that their child is the best, and I did, too, but I kept my mouth shut about it. Every teacher will tell you of the typical "ballet mother" who babbles on about her child's talent, who criticizes the teacher and the other children's ability, who literally thinks and talks as if the child and the parent were one and the same person. This type of parent can only hinder a child's success in whatever he or she is doing. Children, especially young children, are very sensitive to their parents' feelings and the last thing a fledgling dancer needs is this kind of pressure. One of the most important things I have learned in my life is to say very little. Think plenty, but say nothing.

These days, if your child wants to dance, you should encourage her or him. You must give the child every opportunity. You must find the best accredited teacher you can, either by studying the dance magazines, which contain reams of information, or by finding out the name of the teacher who taught a dancer you particularly admire. You can do this through the magazines again, or by looking in any of the various dance encyclopedias. Anyway, once you have chosen a teacher whom you respect, you must place all your faith in that teacher and in your child. There comes a point when you have to let children go. They will either make a success or make a flop—but at this stage it is their responsibility, not yours. I let Margot go the day she was accepted into the Vic-Wells Ballet Company. She was then fourteen years old.

Each year, Miss Bosustow gave a prize to the child who had made the most progress, and Margot won it at the end of her first year. Then there were R.A.D. (Royal Academy of Dancing) exams to take, when, apart from showing the steps she had learned, she had to answer questions about them. When we were at home, I would say to Margot, "What is a *plié*?" and she would promptly reply, "It is a bending of the knees over the toes." And then I would say, "Oh, then what is a *grand battement*?" and again promptly, "It's a throwing up of the leg from the hip," and so on. She remembered everything, but always the day before any exam or performance or competition she would get a temperature and have to stay in bed. Somehow she always managed to recover to do what she had to do. For her Grade I exam she got a mark of 95 out of 100; Grade II the next year, 85; Grade III, 70.

Margot, of course, was still very young. She loved dancing; that was obvious. She didn't much care for the hard work, but she loved performing and dressing up, and she seemed to understand that one was necessary for the other.

Miss Bosustow's classes were in no way advanced. She was a cheerful and encouraging teacher. She corrected her students gently but firmly and never pushed a child beyond his or her limits.

After those three years, my husband's business dictated that we move to China, via the United States. We stayed in Louisville, Kentucky, for a time, and I enrolled Margot in a co-educational public school. She had difficulty making friends there, so it was not long before I started looking for a ballet school to supplement her education. I pursued this interest basically because it was clear that Margot loved it, and it was obviously something that she did well. By this time, she considered it a natural part of her life, although it never entered her head, or mine, that one day it would become her career. I found only one school in the telephone directory, and when Margot and I went along to watch a class we were surprised by what we saw. First of all, there was very little discipline, and students of a similar age to Margot were involved in doing high kicks and splits. It was also clear that they hadn't learned the basic ballet positions properly. I made up my mind then that no classes were better than bad classes.

Doubtless times have changed, and I am sure that one can now find reputable teachers in Louisville—or anywhere else, for that matter. The fact remains, however, that it is still very easy to stumble onto a bad one.

From Kentucky we moved to Tientsin, in China. There I was lucky to find a Russian lady called Madame Svetlanova, who had a ballet school. Although the styles were different, her classes were very like those of Miss Bosustow and so Margot resumed her study. She was quite happy and enjoyed herself there.

At home we started to arrange dances ourselves to a portable gramophone we had brought from England. We spent a lot of time choosing suitable records. Before we left, Margot got her first press notice for a tambourine dance she had made up herself. She was the hit of the performance and obviously gave it her all.

Later, after a brief visit back to London, we moved to Shanghai, and it was there that ballet for us became less of a pleasant pastime and more of a consuming interest.

I was, by then, a keen subscriber to the *Dancing Times*, Britain's leading dance magazine. It used to arrive every month by boat, and Margot and I devoured each issue as it arrived. Through it we learned of the ever-increasing popularity of ballet back home, of the brilliant partnership of Anton Dolin and Alicia Markova, and of the emergence in 1933 of the so-called "baby ballerinas" Baronova, Toumanova, and Riabouchinska. Margot also took great interest in the all-England dance competitions in which she had been so successful. In the ballet world, certainly, Shanghai was a long, long way from London. . . .

As soon as we found a flat, we settled down and made new friends, amongst whom was an Englishwoman called Mrs. Brae. It was she and her daughter

June who inadvertently pushed us into the next step of Margot's eventual career. June was absolutely mad about dancing, and Mrs. Brae in turn worshiped her daughter. She had found three Russian dancing teachers for June and an American friend to study with. One was a woman who had a studio; the other two were men with no studios. Undaunted, Mrs. Brae cleared her sitting room, had a *barre* installed, and she herself played the piano during the lessons.

As soon as I met Mrs. Brae and learned about all of this, I asked whether Margot could join in as well. We were very pleased when she readily agreed. The next day we all went to the studio of the woman teacher. After watching I decided that, according to our standards, she was ruining the children by letting them do movements that their muscles were not then ready or strong enough to take. I also noticed that she was letting June turn her legs out from the knee and not from the hip, which was a very serious fault. I told Mrs. Brae all of this and said that I would not allow Margot to take the class, and advised her to take June out of it as well. Fortunately, she was impressed with my knowledge and none of us went there again.

Of the two men, one, Gontcharov, was a fully trained Russian émigré from the Bolshoi Theatre, in Moscow, so we were very lucky to find him. The other, Elirov, was an older, plump man who had never been a dancer himself, although his wife had. He evidently had watched a lot and now taught what he called *plastique* dancing. It was a sort of cross between Isadora Duncan, classical, and any other type of dance he had seen whose movements pleased him. I thought he was doing no harm, if not much good. June loved his class and we were interested in it as well, for the exercises he gave were generally graceful and soft,

and not likely to strain any muscles. Of the two, however, there was no question that Gontcharov was the
better teacher.

June was an exceptionally keen and bright student, and her interest in these classes fired Margot's
ambition to do even better. Margot never could stand
to be number two in anything. . . . Naturally, by
then we were all good friends, and the Braes' attitude
strongly influenced ours and vice versa. June was two
years older than Margot. She was about fourteen at
the time and Margot twelve.

After a while, Mrs. Brae, following June's desire
to "get on," decided that she would take her daughter
back to London to study with the famous Nicholas
Legat, who at one time partnered Pavlova and who
was reputed to be an excellent teacher. Margot was by
now fourteen and anxious to join them.

This led me to one of the most difficult decisions I
ever had to make. My husband's work was in Shanghai, and taking Margot back to London would mean
leaving him for an extended period of time, which
naturally was upsetting for both of us. We discussed
the situation at great length, and it was finally agreed
that as Margot had progressed as far as she could in
Shanghai, the only place to find out if indeed she had
a particular talent for dancing was back home. We decided that if Margot and I traveled to London a few
months in advance of his next period of home leave, it
would allow us time to assess her potential before he
arrived for a united family holiday.

Once we arrived in London, I decided that the
Legat classes, which June was attending, were far too
advanced for Margot. All the students were in their
early teens. Some were good, some not so good, but
one thing I didn't like was that the teacher seldom cor-

rected them. I considered this extremely important, because if you don't receive correction when you are young, things become much more difficult later on.

From studying the dance magazines, I decided that the teacher whom we should next go and see was Princess Serafine Astafieva, who had taught our most famous dancers, Alicia Markova and Anton Dolin. I found out where she lived and made an appointment. It was a fascinating and historic house in the King's Road, Chelsea, and still stands there, isolated, as it awaits a modern building development that is due to surround it on three sides. Its name, The Pheasantry, recalls its origins when Chelsea was a country village.

The interview was initially discouraging, to say the least. There sat Astafieva, huddled next to a stove in a small dark room whose walls were replete with Russian tapestries. She was old, and very obviously ill, and when I asked her if there was any chance of her teaching my daughter, she refused categorically, stating that she didn't want any more students. I persisted, pleading that I had brought my child six thousand miles, all the way from China, to study with her as she had been responsible for Markova and Dolin! "They don't care; they never come to see me," she said. It wasn't true, but she was filled with Russian gloom. In the end, however, she gave in. She dismissed us with a curt "O.K., I look. Come tomorrow."

Margot loved Astafieva from the start. She was an inspired teacher and her lessons full of dance movements, as opposed to the rather dry exercises that some teachers make out of ballet. One of the hallmarks of a great teacher is the ability to see exactly and immediately why a student has difficulty executing certain steps, and to suggest adjustments to the part of the body concerned in order to facilitate the movement.

Astafieva was a genius at this, and she made Margot's work much easier for her.

I enjoyed the classes, as spectator, every bit as much as Margot, but I realized that since she was approaching fifteen, it had come to the point where I had to know if all this training was going to lead somewhere; I just couldn't continue to spend the time, money, and effort on my daughter's occupation if it wasn't. The only place I could find out if she had the talent for a theatrical future was a place where that talent might be used—a ballet company.

When I discussed with Astafieva the idea of taking Margot to the Vic-Wells Ballet School, she was indignant at first. Possibly she couldn't bear the thought of relinquishing another student. Anyway, she finally agreed that perhaps it was the best thing to do. Margot found all this very difficult to accept, as she didn't think she was ready and she was very happy where she was. However, she took my word for it.

Unaware of what was to happen, we went along to the Sadler's Wells Theatre unarmed with practice clothes or ballet shoes. And so it was that Margot had to audition barefoot and in her petticoat. After ten minutes she was accepted into the school, and soon afterward it was Ninette de Valois, the director of the company, who took charge of her dancing career. I was no longer actively involved and at first I felt frightened, and then let down, but as I said, there comes a point when you have to let them go, and I did.

I shall never forgot the excitement when, four weeks later, we received a postcard asking Margot to attend a rehearsal for a corps-de-ballet role in the snowflake scene of the ballet *The Nutcracker*. That meant that she was really IN! She had got her toe on the bottom rung of the ladder, and I had made the correct decision after all.

The Mother

Nowadays, people see me in a theatre and they exclaim, "How proud you must be of your daughter." Well, I am very happy with my daughter's success! I am happy that she has been able to give so many people such great pleasure—but my grandma used to say that "Pride comes before a fall"—and falls are bad for dancers!

PART TWO

When a man has been guilty of a mistake,
either in ordering his own affairs, or in
directing those of State, or in commanding an
army, do we not always say: So-and-so has
made a false step in this affair? And can
making a false step derive from anything
but lack of skill in dancing?

—MOLIÈRE (1622–73)

TYPES OF DANCE

BALLET

Ballet is a word that can cause some confusion when one is talking of dance. It is used in various contexts to mean different things. It originates from *ballo* in Italian and *bal* in French, meaning dance in the sense of "a dance" or "a ball"; that is to say, a social occasion at which people dance. The Italian word *balletto* was used in the sixteenth century for a series of social dances usually performed by, but not limited to, couples.

In the sixteenth and seventeenth centuries, some of these social occasions became so elaborate that they included entertainments of music, poetry, and dance, somewhat like a lavish cabaret at a private party performed by the host and his friends. In France, this entertainment came to be called a *ballet*. When these entertainments moved from the great halls of royal palaces into real theatres, the dance element was developed and eventually separated from the speech or poetry. It retained the name *ballet*. So, first of all, ballet means a stage performance of dance. It can be any kind of dance.

When ballet first moved into the professional theatre, it began to evolve a system of technique based quite simply on the social dances of the day. These social or ballroom dances were complicated; every respectable young man and woman spent a considerable amount of time perfecting the many difficult steps and learning the formation of each dance. For ease and grace, it was necessary to turn the feet out toward the side—as a fencer does in order to move rapidly in any direction with utmost control. In the theatre, it was only a question of elaborating these same steps with more intricate footwork, and adding more leaps and jumps and turns. Lo and behold! There was the style or technique of dancing that we now call ballet. So it is really nothing more than a legitimate development of the minuet and other eighteenth-century social dances. What makes it seem so far removed from everyday life is the footwear. Whereas ballroom, tap, jazz, and folk dancing can be done in normal shoes or boots, and modern dance is done in bare feet, only ballet dancers and gymnasts wear close-fitting little slippers with soft soles and no heels; and the women's toeshoes could be regarded as almost freakish if one were not accustomed to them.

But as more of the workaday clothes of dancers and athletes, such as tights, leotards, track suits, and so forth, are adapted for casual fashion wear, so ballet becomes less and less remote from everyday life—almost back to where it started!

Another confusion is caused by references to Russian ballet, English ballet, American ballet, and so on. It is sometimes hard to know what is meant. People ask me which training is best, but in fact all ballet training is basically the same. There are, however, big differences in detail, and choice is a matter of personal taste. English training produces an effect of effortlessness; American training develops speed and agility. The expression "Russian ballet method" does not have any precise meaning. Before the Russian Revolution the style of training in Moscow differed from that in St. Petersburg: Moscow dancers were more flamboyant; St. Petersburg dancers were softer. Soviet Russian training, which is different again in style, now accentuates high leaps and strength. Both the Leningrad and the Moscow schools have evolved and moved closer to each other but still retain individual characteristics. In spite of all these variations in detail, the technique is standard and universal. It presents no problems for ballet dancers of one nationality to perform in the ballet company of any other country.

"Classical ballet" is another confusing term. These days it is sometimes used to mean the type of training that we call ballet, and it is also applied to those ballets created in Russia during the late nineteenth century that are performed, either complete or in excerpts, in versions that are more or less related to their original productions. *Swan Lake*, *The Nutcracker*, *The Sleeping Beauty*, *Don Quixote*, *La Bayadère*, and *Le Corsaire* are the ones seen most frequently outside Russia, and only the first four of those are shown in their entirety. (*Giselle*, a French ballet, dates from an earlier period, the 1840s, and is classified as a "romantic" ballet. *Coppélia* is a French *demi-caractère* ballet, dating from 1870, that can now be called "a classic.")

A BALLET CLASS

A ballet class is divided into two sections: the first warms up the body and prepares it for the second part, which is the practice of sequences of steps. The whole class prepares the dancer to rehearse a ballet and the rehearsal prepares the dancer for a performance. (In a way, each performance is a rehearsal for the perform-

ance that will follow; but not without starting again
at the beginning with class!)

I talk about preparing the body because the material to be trained consists of muscles, tendons, lig-
aments, joints, and so forth. These must become so
familiar with each movement that they can be said to
have learned them. But they are not selective; they
will learn anything they repeat often enough. Without the mind constantly sending instructions, check-
ing and correcting, they will just as likely learn the
movements wrongly. It is an annoying fact that the
wrong way to do an exercise is initially the easiest
way, and muscles, being lazy by nature, look for
whatever gives them the least trouble. In the long
run, this results in more trouble, because ballet technique is so scientifically devised that the more correctly it is performed the easier it becomes.

If we start at the performance and look back, the
function of the class may be clearer. A dancer on the
stage—a very professional one—looks completely at
ease; the movements flow one into another apparently
without thought, and one could easily believe the
dancer improvises as the mood takes him. But watch
the movement carefully; he throws one leg forward,
rises in the air with the other leg behind him; he lands
on the first leg without a jolt (the leg behind still in
the air), then goes immediately and smoothly into
another movement. That one jump has taken hours
and hours of preparation repeated over several years.
In performance, the public is hardly aware of the two
little steps that have prepared his force for the take-
off, or of the arms moving simultaneously in their
own directions contributing to the preparatory force.
They notice the arm thrust forward at the height of
the jump: it is the arm opposite to the leg that is in
front; it has helped the dancer to rise off the ground,

it helps to propel him forward and, after he has landed, it moves in coordination with the rest of the body toward the next important effort.

Coordination is the keynote. Each arm, each leg, each foot, the head, and shoulders—all have their part to play and the exact moment to play it. It all happens so quickly, like the different musical instruments of an orchestra combining to produce a bar of a symphony, that it would be impossible for the brain to think of so many different things at once. The body has to be trained until everything responds simultaneously to a single impulse from the brain.

The first section of the class concentrates on warming muscles, working tendons to make them supple, and loosening joints. It consists of exercises that are basic to the types of movement that compose the second part of the class.

All the exercises are done in the "turned-out" position, which is fundamental to every movement in ballet technique. As I have already explained, the legs are turned out from the hip joint, which means that the kneecaps face toward the sides instead of forward as is normal. In order to work in this position without undue strain during the warming up, the dancer holds on to the *barre*.

Beginners usually face the *barre* and hold with both hands, then progress to the normal manner of holding with the left hand while working the right leg, then turning to hold with the right hand while exercising the other leg.

There are five positions of the feet, but one of them—third position—is really a modified fifth position and is used only by beginners until they can achieve fifth.

First and fifth positions are "closed" because the feet touch each other. In first position the heels touch and the toes point out to the sides. In fifth position one foot is in front of the other so that they cross completely, heels aligned with toes, like sardines in a tin. (In third position the feet cross only halfway.)

Second and fourth positions are "open" because the feet are separated. In second position the feet are on the same line, as in first position, but this time there is a space between the heels. In fourth position one foot is in front of the other and they cross as in fifth position, but this time separated by a space.

(If the dancer is not facing squarely to one wall of the room but facing one of the corners, the second position is called *écarté* and the fifth or fourth [or third] position becomes fifth or fourth [or third] crossed or open, depending on which foot is in front of the other.)

The foot of the working leg is always pointed in classical ballet, whether it is resting on the floor (*pointe tendu*) or raised in the air. (Choreographers can and do put flexed feet into their ballets.)

When the dancer stands on one leg so that the other leg is free to move in the air (or free to move just touching the floor but bearing no weight), the leg she is standing on is called the "supporting leg" and the other leg is called the "working leg." The entire sole of the foot of the supporting leg or of both feet can be on the floor, or the heel can be raised so that the dancer is standing on the ball of the foot (called *demi-pointe*, or half-point). Girls wearing toeshoes can also stand on the tips of the toes, or on point.

The dancer is always in one of the four basic positions or on her way from one of them to another. This is true whether she is standing on one leg or both legs, and whether the leg (or legs) she is stand-

ing on is straight or bent (*plié*). It is true whether
the working leg is resting on the floor or raised in the
air and, if it is raised, whether it is straight (*développé* front or side, *arabesque*) or bent (*attitude*).
The working leg can also be bent with the toe touching the supporting leg at the ankle (*sur le cou-de-
pied*) or at the midcalf or knee (*passé*), as it is during
a pirouette. And, finally, it is true when both feet are
off the floor—that is, during jumps.

The movement of the legs to any position never
displaces the hips, and the legs are always turned out.
Some movements of the leg take place only from the
knee down, without moving the thigh at all (for example, *rond de jambe en l'air*).

All the foot and leg positions have their appropriate standard and alternate arm positions. The movement of arms from one position to another is called
port de bras, which is also the name given to various
exercises in which these movements are practiced.
These exercises can be done with or without moving
the legs.

Each composite position of feet, legs, and arms
also has its appropriate standard positions of the torso.
And there are also appropriate positions for the head.
Even in movement there is always a precise place in
which all the components should be at any given
moment. To achieve this coordination, the dancer
needs precise control.

Control requires strength; strength is developed by
repetition. (The French word for rehearsal is *répétition*.) Muscles and tendons have to be prepared by
gentle stages to accept the enormous variety of movements.

All the exercises done at the *barre* are either part
or the whole of steps that will be done in the center of
the room.

There are exercises for:

1. Bending the knees with the weight on both legs;
   and also,
   Bending one knee, the other foot touching the
   ground without bearing weight, or off
   the ground.

   PURPOSE:

   to make the tendons supple—Achilles in particular;

   warm the muscles;

   exercise the knee and ankle joints gently;

   strengthen the thigh muscles.

2. Extending one leg to any height, keeping the
   weight on the other leg; and also,
   Transferring the weight from one leg to both, or
   to the other leg—or from both legs to one.

   PURPOSE:

   to stretch and relax muscles;

   exercise foot muscles;

   exercise ankle and hip joints;

   strengthen leg muscles, particularly the thigh.

3. One foot striking against the other ankle or calf.

   PURPOSE:

   to exercise and strengthen the ankle and
   knee joints.

4. Circling one leg on the floor or in the air.

   PURPOSE:

   to exercise and strengthen the hip and knee;

   strengthen the thigh muscles.

5. Raising heels from the floor with the weight on
   one or both legs.

   PURPOSE:

   to strengthen foot muscles.

All these movements are done in an infinite variety of combinations. The exercises performed at the *barre* can last from ten to thirty minutes—or more.

The second section of the class, in the center of the room, is divided into different types of movement:

1. Center practice: repetition of some or all of the *barre* exercises.
2. *Port de bras:* arrangement of arm and torso movements, with or without leg movements.
3. Adagio: arrangement of different sustained movements, mostly standing on one leg.
4. Allegro: small quick movements that slide, jump, travel, change weight, and so on.
5. Pirouettes: all kinds of turns.
6. *Batterie:* all kinds of small jumps in which the feet beat across each other.
7. Elevation: all kinds of high and traveling jumps or turning jumps.
8. *Sur la pointe* (girls): all kinds of steps that rise onto the toes of one or both feet;

   step straight onto the point of one foot;

   hop or jump on the toes (small jumps).

Jumping steps, low or high, can be:

- from both feet, landing on both;
- from both feet, landing on one foot;
- from one foot, landing on both feet;
- from one foot, landing on one foot.

They can be done in one place, can travel, or turn.

Arrangements of steps can include any of the different types of steps mixed together. An arrangement is called an *enchaînement*.

The two sections of class together, *barre* and center, normally last from forty-five minutes (for beginners) to an hour and a half. Children attending class once or twice a week only touch the tip of the iceberg so far as the full range of technique is concerned. The possible combinations and permutations of steps are so infinite that a famous teacher in Russia is said never to have given the same arrangement of steps twice in all his daily classes over many years.

Serious students should have daily classes from the age of twelve—or ten, if possible—because it is impossible to cover all the types of movement *thoroughly* in one class or even in three classes a week. Some teachers plan a general class that covers all the types briefly but concentrates particularly on one different type each day of the week. Others have different systems to insure that students who attend daily work through all the necessary movements each week.

Point practice for girls is best done in an extra fifteen or twenty minutes at the end of class and in some additional classes once or twice a week. It is not, of course, for beginners but for intermediate and advanced students.

Dancing on point is an extension of the normal classwork and does not include a different range of steps. It is usual to do the daily class in soft shoes or very old point shoes, and then to change into newer toeshoes to practice steps selected especially to strengthen the dancer's technique in that area.

There are certain steps that cannot be done on point—obviously the high jumps are impossible because the push-off from toe tips gives a very limited elevation, and landing from any height on the toes would be akin to an unsuccessful parachute drop; even if a dancer's knees and feet were physically strong enough to withstand the impact, the aesthetic effect would be hideous. Small hops and jumps on point are perfectly possible and form an important part of advanced technique; pirouettes are enhanced by turning on the point of the foot, because it approximates more closely the point of a spinning top.

If there are boys and girls in class together, the girls do point work at the end when the boys do turns and jumps that are not part of the girls' repertoire, as well as steps of high elevation.

A girl's point class is additional to the daily class, and concentrates entirely on point dancing as used on the stage. Boys and girls also have to learn partnering. In this, the brunt of the work is taken by the boy, but the girl must learn to help as much as she can by not throwing herself off balance and expecting to be retrieved smoothly or making it impossible for her partner not to drop her from a lift. These are called pas-de-deux, or supported-adagio, classes and, like all the others, last about an hour and a half. The girls must wear toeshoes because the balance is different on point than on half-point.

Ballet training has changed quite a lot during this century. It now concentrates on developing the whole body rather than primarily the legs and arms. The old-fashioned training tended to overwork the legs and overdeveloped the calf muscles. Nowadays good training actually improves the dancer's figure.

The well-trained dancer is one who has achieved masterly control over his or her body and is free to employ it as a truly expressive medium of art.

MODERN DANCE

Modern dance differs radically from ballet in concept, practice, and attitude. As we have seen, ballet is a

style of dancing based on a universal and set vocabulary of steps and positions. The ballet dancer, through years of training, learns this vocabulary, and the choreographer uses it in seemingly endless combinations to produce the desired effect.

Modern dance has no such universal vocabulary. It is more natural in concept and its movements are dictated by the individual artist-choreographer to suit his or her choreographic needs. There is no one all-encompassing style of modern dance, for there are as many styles as there are choreographers. The constant factor in this art does not lie in technique, but rather in motivation. In all modern dance, the movement must come from within. The purpose of a modern dance class therefore is to prepare the dancer's body to be receptive to the intensely personal creative urges of the choreographer.

Modern dance has its roots in Central Europe and America in the early part of this century, at a time when ballet dancing in those areas was regarded as meaningless, rigid, and dead. In Switzerland and Germany a small group of experimentalists gathered around Rudolf von Laban, who studied the relation of movement to religion, science, astrology, medicine, psychology, education, and so forth, producing many original theories and inspiring others to innovative dance creation.

At the same time, Isadora Duncan, with her efforts to return dance to the ancient Greek ideals of natural beauty, led many American followers to search out fresh sources of inspiration. Almost contemporary with her was Ruth St. Denis, who was more involved in the ancient mysteries of Egypt, India, and the East. She had a superb sense of theatre and took infinite pains to create an appropriate atmosphere for each of her solo Oriental dances. Unlike Isadora Duncan, who danced alone or with a background of girls, St. Denis chose to work with a young man who shared her idealism, and they formed a partnership that led to their marriage. He was Ted Shawn, and it was as a result of his influence that, in 1915, they co-founded the first modern dance company and school in America. They called it Denishawn.

From its inception, the Denishawn company was concerned with production. Duncan had been content to present her art to the European public simply and directly. Ted Shawn was sufficiently sensitive to the taste of the American public to know that it required more elaborate presentation. In that sense, the company was commercial. They relied heavily on ornate costumes, décor, and lighting to present their highly stylized interpretations of Egyptian and Indian gods and goddesses. On the other hand, they took dance seriously. They were intent on presenting to the public an art form capable of expressing what St. Denis often referred to as "the most noble thoughts of man."

Some of the most famous names in contemporary modern dance were launched through the Denishawn company. Among these were Doris Humphrey, Charles Weidman, and the most famous modern dancer-choreographer of all, Martha Graham.

The new generation was primarily concerned with getting back to basics. All of them rejected, in the end, the stylized approach to dance they had been taught. The two World Wars played a role in shaping their concepts. It was time for American dance to assert its independence. Out went all the elaborate costumes and productions—in came simple and severe long dresses for women and workmen's shirts and trousers for men. Modern dance, if it was to succeed, needed a radical approach, even if it meant sacrificing public popularity. The new choreography reflected the need to express personal experience as it related to current society; it also reflected a new concern for body rhythms.

Martha Graham developed her theory of contraction and release to correspond to the natural body movements of inhaling and exhaling. Doris Humphrey considered all movement to be a matter of equilibrium—of balance and imbalance—and so she developed her theory of fall and recovery.

Graham looked inward. She was concerned with making visible the "interior landscape." Her choreography was sharp and angular in the beginning and full of percussive attack. Later it became somewhat modified by more lyrical movement, but what was present then and is still present today is a kind of inner alertness, a stressed tension whereby the dancer always seems poised on the brink of danger and discovery.

She developed and refined her own technique, based on her theory of contraction and release of energy, of which a striking feature is the impulse starting at the core of the body, the spine, and flowing out to the ends of the limbs. Her choreography explored and continues to explore all forms of human emotion and awareness. Her works are many-layered —full of psychological and symbolic significance. Her themes are many and varied, but she seems to have found a great deal of inspiration in ritual, in the American heritage, and in Greek myth, which, like Duncan, she felt was the prototype for all human feeling. Throughout her life, she has been committed to the use of new musical scores and starkly modern designs to accompany her work.

Martha Graham is an American genius whose work is respected and performed all over the world. She retired from the performing stage in 1969 at the age of seventy-five, but continues to be an active choreographer, teacher, and company director of the school she founded in 1927. The technique she evolved is certainly the most popular one ever devised for modern dance, and it will continue to live and develop in the hands of the myriad dancer-choreographer teachers who have passed through her company. Among the many are Anna Sokolow, Alwin Nikolais, Paul Taylor, and Merce Cunningham.

Whereas Graham looked inward, to the "interior landscape" of the human soul, Doris Humphrey looked primarily at the relationship of the individual to outside forces. Her works were broadly heroic in concept and represented, more often than not, a triumph over adversity. Unlike many modern dancers of her generation, she had a good foundation in ballet training. She also co-choreographed several pieces with Ruth St. Denis for the Denishawn company. Perhaps this is why she was not as violent and radical in her attitudes toward the contemporary idiom as was Martha Graham.

Humphrey left Denishawn in 1928 with Charles Weidman, and together they formed a company and school dedicated to developing her technique based on her principle of fall and recovery. She wrote a book about this called *The Art of Making Dances*, and it is now respected as one of the great treatises on the subject.

The Humphrey-Weidman school and company built a repertory richly varied in style and theme, but always true to the premise that emotion comes before movement. Humphrey's choreographic talent ranged from simple studies based on nature to choreographically more difficult subjects like *The Shakers*, about an American religious sect, and abstract works danced to the music of Bach and Grieg.

Weidman was a great teacher as well as a fine choreographer. He had a subtle sense of humor and he tended to provide lighter elements in the repertory, some of them semi-autobiographical and others based on the books of James Thurber.

The Humphrey-Weidman students were encouraged to retain their individualism, and so their disciples, such as José Limón, Sybil Shearer, and Ann Halprin, went on to develop unique personal styles, never carbon copies of their mentors.

This short review is by no means comprehensive, but from it we see how modern dance evolved and how different it is from ballet in practice and concept.

There are other technical differences that have not been discussed. Ballet is based on turned-out positions. That is why the ballet dancer, in order to train the muscles, must study while comparatively young. In modern dance the turnout is not so extreme, and because point work is not used at all, it is possible for the prospective dancer to commence training at a later age.

The dancer's relation to the ground is one of modern dance's most important features. Whereas in ballet the dancer is concerned with lightness, elevation, and defiance of gravity, the modern dancer uses the ground as a source of stability and strength. The back, which is held firm and strong in ballet, can be rounded and supple in modern dance.

These days the two art forms have a mutual respect for one another. The younger generation of modern dancers does not feel the same hostility toward ballet as the founding generation did; many actually take ballet training along with their modern classes because they recognize that this kind of formal training adds discipline and strength and makes them

more accomplished artists. Also, many essentially modern choreographers work within the ballet idiom, among them Glen Tetley, Alvin Ailey, and Twyla Tharp. Likewise, ballet choreographers are increasingly influenced by modern movement.

Although completely different in nature, there is no doubt that ballet and modern dance have had and will continue to have a considerable effect on one another.

A MODERN DANCE CLASS

Of all the modern dancers in the world today, Martha Graham has progressed the furthest in establishing a set technique and a method for training the dancer's body. This method is taught in many professional dance schools. While it is not practicable to describe fully all the exercises used in a Graham class, it is possible to discuss the theory behind the technical training she advocates. She believes that all exercises should be based on the structure of the body, and that all of them should be extensions of its inherent physical capabilities. As such, there should be no artificial or forced movements. She also believes that as dance is motion, all exercises should be based on the body in motion as its natural state. She believes that training has three purposes: to strengthen, to liberate, and to prepare the body and soul to accept spontaneity of action.

All exercises in a Graham class are in the form of theme and variation. The exercise starts with a specific area simplified of all extraneous movement or embellishment, and then widens in scope to incorporate the use of the entire body.

The Graham class is divided into four main categories: floor exercises, exercises standing in one place, elevation exercises, and finally exercises for falls.

The floor exercises comprise leg extensions, stretching, and back exercise. They incorporate her theory of contraction and release to correspond with the natural body rhythm of inhaling and exhaling. There should be no forcing of any movement in these exercises. Strength must be allowed to develop slowly and gradually. These exercises are meant to prepare the body for the following standing and elevation sections.

The second section involves all exercises for the legs, hips, feet, and finally turns in place. In all *pliés,* the moderate turned-out position is used. As with ballet, in the *plié* work close attention is paid to the knees and feet. The movement must come from the hip. The knees must not be allowed to roll inward.

The next section involves exercises for elevation. These include leaps, skips, turns in the air, runs, and jumping in place. All previous exercise should have strengthened the body sufficiently to perform these without strain.

The final section concerns fall and recovery. The dancer learns to fall from various positions using different rhythms. The whole process should be a means of affirmation. The body never remains on the floor, but rises to an upright position as part of the exercise. The motivation must come from within, and on no account must the spine or the knees strike the floor. The energy must be contained in the legs and the arms.

Graham believes that her classes should not be intended only for professional use. She believes that they can be of serious emotional and physical benefit both to the untrained adult and to the child.

SHOW DANCE

The term "show dance" applies to dance in the so-called lighter forms of theatrical entertainment such as musicals, revues, cabaret, and any associated presentations of that nature. The types of dancing called for in these entertainments can be just about anything and everything that the dancers can do. Show dancers are also often expected to sing. Training includes tap dancing and jazz, some modern dance and ballet.

The big difference between working in this medium or specializing in ballet or modern dance is that whereas the dance companies present a changing repertoire with the same group of performers, show dancers are engaged for the run of one particular show. The variety of roles in a changing repertoire allows for a slow but continuous artistic development. The dancer in a show must repeat the same performance endlessly with unflagging energy and enthusiasm, which requires extraordinary discipline but does not reward him or her with a sense of progress.

A JAZZ CLASS

The purpose of a jazz class is to introduce a supple strength into the body coupled with a strong sense of rhythmic coordination. It is aimed at the professional dancer who works in the musical theatre, film, and television business. However, it has become increasingly popular with the nonprofessional because it is such a pleasant and enjoyable way of toning and firming the body, as well as keeping fit in general.

There are many different types of jazz class. As with modern dance, the technique that is taught depends on the teacher. As there is no *barre* work and only a limited use of the turned-out positions, most professional dancers supplement their jazz training with ballet classes.

A typical jazz class is divided into four sections: stationary isolation exercises; floor exercises; jumps, turns, and balancing exercises; final combination.

The purpose of isolation exercises is to train the dancer to be able to use each part of the body independently. The dancer faces front, feet parallel, about eighteen inches apart. In this section, he or she works on the head, the neck, the shoulders, the rib cage, the hips, and the legs and feet. Each part of the body from the head to the hips is exercised in two ways: first the slow continuous roll front, right, back, left, followed by the more static right, center; left, center; front, center; back, center. Then comes a series of slow kneebends, half and full, in comfortable, only partly turned-out first and second positions.

The purpose of floor exercises is to work on the extension of the legs, control of the back, and strengthening of the abdominal muscles. The dancer sits on the floor with the soles of his feet placed together. He holds his ankles with his hands and bounces forward, first with a straight back and then with a curved one so that his head almost touches his feet. Then he combines these two movements into one continuous flowing action. Then he extends his legs, feet pointing outward, and goes through a series of pointing and flexing of the feet. This is followed by a series of sit-ups, and other exercises designed to tighten the abdominal muscles.

These two sections constitute the warm-up part of the class. No further complex movement should ever be attempted before all these exercises have been suc-

cessfully completed. Otherwise, the dancer risks serious damage to his muscles.

The next series of exercises concerns elevation and
turns. In all types of jumping, the force must come
from the whole leg and not just the ankle. The movement must first start with a kneebend. In turning, the
dancer must learn to spot—that is, to focus on an individual point in space—in order to avoid dizziness.

The final section is generally a jazz routine improvised by the teacher, varying in degrees of difficulty and utilizing the different exercises taught in
class. Sometimes, the routine is built on from class
to class.

Jazz classes are available in the beginner, intermediate, and advanced levels and last from an hour to an hour and a half.

FOLK DANCE

Originally, folk dances were the traditional dances of each country and each region, sometimes of each village, throughout the world. They were handed down from one generation to the next for centuries, evolving a little on the way but basically unchanged. Children simply picked them up by copying their elders. They learned the dances in the same way that they learned to talk, and had no need of teachers.

The pattern of modern life in big cities breaks up that natural cycle, and a conscious effort has to be made by ethnic groups to preserve their cultural traditions. This happens most frequently when immigrants in a new country feel the need to maintain the memory and customs of their homeland; but, generally speaking, the natural folk dance is rapidly dying out.

Luckily, dance conservationists seek out and record what has not yet been lost altogether, and many folk dance societies are formed to encourage the continuation of old traditions. ·

NATIONAL DANCE

In the nineteenth century, ballet introduced national dances to add variety to a long evening of otherwise pure ballet dancing. The Polish mazurka and cracovienne, the Hungarian czardas, various Spanish and Italian and Russian dances turned up frequently, using traditional steps and formations rearranged for

the stage. (The dances of more distant lands were not known in detail, so the wildest imagination went into the creation of Turkish, Scottish, or Chinese scenes.)

Once ballet had shown how well folk art adapted to the stage, it was an easy step to engage whole troupes of dancers in lively and colorful presentations of the national dance heritage. In this century such dance companies are regarded as contributors to international understanding, because music and dance, like painting, have no language barrier. The timeless dances of remote villages that were once accessible only to intrepid travelers now come to those who sit comfortably in the cushioned theatre seats of their home cities.

SPANISH AND INDIAN DANCE

Obviously, Spanish dancing is a type of ethnic dance. I only mention it separately because there is such a variety and richness in the dances of Spain, both classical and flamenco, that they are a study in themselves. The same is true of the dance of India, which is the most ancient dance tradition of all and includes several different styles or schools. Remote as the two countries may seem, there is, in fact, a very distant relationship between Indian dance and that of the Spanish gypsies.

Spanish training naturally includes the playing of castanets, the exact origin of which would be hard to determine. The use of little wooden clappers was common for dancers in Egypt under the pharaohs, in ancient Greece, and in the Middle East as a whole. Turkish and other Oriental dancers also used tiny cymbals on thumb and finger to emphasize rhythm and add a charming accent to the musical accompaniment.

Spanish flamenco is the dance of gypsies who traveled from the East through Europe via North Africa to Spain, where they settled in the caves around Granada. Their concentration on stamping and footwork bears witness to their dance's long-lost origins in India, where the feet make their own soft rhythm as they shake their anklets of tiny bells. Spanish classical dancing is restrained in style, as it was the social dance of noblemen and courtiers in earlier times.

Femininity and grace are natural to Indian women, and it is a pity that the study of their dance is not more available in the Occident, for it would be very rewarding. At the moment, its study almost requires traveling to India itself. Very few dancers have opened schools in the West and we have too little knowledge of the art and its significance. Perhaps the religious foundations of this dance, being so alien to us, have made it a study for the specialists rather than the general public. Many Indian dances are like long narrative ballets depicting sagas of the gods.

Possibly one day Japanese and Chinese classical dance will also be taught in the West. What better way to understand more of alien people than to participate in their culture and arts?

The end

SOCIAL DANCE

Social dancing is ballroom dancing, but since it is as frequently performed on a tiny area of floor in a cramped disco or nightclub as in the traditional spacious ballroom, "social" seems a more appropriate name for this style of dancing. It is a hybrid that is neither an artificial theatre art like ballet nor a completely natural form like folk dance.

Social dance originates one way or another in folk dance, but is adapted for completely different circumstances. It is really a commodity like fashion, which is affected by social and political conditions and provides a livelihood for those engaged in its trade. The history of social dance is a very fascinating study and one that I think is a little neglected.

Social dance is within the reach of everyone. Amateur ballroom-dancing competitions are very distinguished. They are extremely well organized and give a great deal of pleasure to the participants and spectators alike, as they are quite beautiful to watch. The Brazilian samba schools provide somewhat of a parallel in the degree of time and hard work that go into the making of a good team of amateur dancers.

There is a great importance in amateur dancing, whether competitive or not. It is contact with the fundamental and natural roots of our existence. People who live in big cities are deprived, consciously or unconsciously, of those almost indefinable things on which our human sensitivity feeds, like the first breath of morning country air imperceptibly scented by dew; the glint of late afternoon sun through pale green leaves; the whiff of wood smoke; or even the distant sound of barking carried across fields. A million little bonuses of nature are denied the city dweller; his subconscious is undernourished and his need for art is greater than that of country people.

Some people's senses are deprived and they need the visual and auditory arts; others are deprived physically—the journey to work by subway or bus is no substitute for a brisk country walk. The physical and emotional enjoyment of dancing, unrelated to the responsibilities of stage performance, is one way of compensating for some of the stresses caused by concrete-jungle living. At the present time, for instance,

hundreds of thousands of young people everywhere
are finding an antidote to the normal frustrations of
their age in disco dancing, which is the current dance
mania, comparable to the polka of the mid-nineteenth
century or the Charleston of the twenties.

THE STUDENT

A student of dance is a person working seriously to make a career in the art. As a profession, dance has its hazards like any other art. Nevertheless I believe it to be the best and most agreeable life, because people who perform on the stage enjoy some sort of special magic not really found anywhere else.

No one should go into the theatre who is not suited to the way of life. Regular hours and free weekends are unknown. None of the arts can be regarded purely as a job to be carried out within preordained hours. It is necessary to have some sense of perfection and the will to do whatever is required to give of one's best. This is something that dancers in general do have, and it is one of the things that make dance an agreeable career, because it is satisfying to work with people one respects. Whether the work is hard or not is difficult to say, and anyway what does it matter so long as it is enjoyable?

I am always surprised by the number of people who ask what dancers do to keep fit for the strenuous life they lead. The answer is, of course, just the reverse —it is the strenuous life that keeps them fit. Students do make efforts these days to be slim, and probably watch their diets, but I cannot believe it right to take so much exercise without sufficient protein and such other nutrients as the body needs—which may differ with each individual. To project a performance to the public takes energy and enthusiasm, two things that don't come easily to the undernourished. It is not sufficient on stage to go through steps and movements as in a classroom. The same steps become something quite different when they are used to express the theme and character of the choreography; they must be transformed and given to the public as a "performance" and carry with them that magic which is the secret of the theatre. No one can say exactly what makes one performer stand out from all the others and catch the attention of every member of the public. It is not only a case of dancing better than the others but also of deep concentration, and involvement in the meaning of what is danced.

Of necessity, students must work to the utmost to perfect their control and strength of movement, but beyond that aspect they must not overlook what dancing is all about. The classroom is never more than a preparation for the stage, and that is where judgment is made.

It may be that some students will go instead into other branches of dance, such as teaching or notation, but that does not alter what I have said. Teachers who have not themselves been professional dancers must still regard the classroom as only a preparation for the stage. For why else do we learn to dance if not to give beauty and pleasure to others? Admittedly, it is a vanity to try to attract the attention of the public to ourselves, but it is not as easy as it seems. The stage demands full value, and the public won't look at those who offer a perfunctory performance. Nothing less than our best means putting our hearts and souls into what we are doing.

THE DANCER

Professional dancers, like other human beings, come in all shapes and sizes, but there are certain requisites, both physical and mental, that are important if one is to succeed in this fickle profession.

Good health, a strong constitution, and a well-proportioned body are necessary. Height also is an important consideration, especially for girls, because point shoes add at least six inches. Ideally, girls should be between five feet two inches and five feet six inches, and although there is really no fixed height for boys, they should in general be between five feet seven inches and six feet. Of course there are exceptions to this rule; in fact, at times nature perversely provides a surfeit of tall ballerinas at the same time as a glut of short male dancers. Generally speaking, the long-legged dancers excel in slow, graceful movements, while the smaller dancers dazzle with their speed.

It is difficult to predict with certainty the eventual height of a twelve-year-old, but bone measurements and the height of the parents may provide quite substantial clues.

Apart from these purely physical qualities, ideally a dancer should be determined, receptive, patient, and possess a strong sense of self-awareness. He or she must be able to accept criticism readily, for this is a common element in a dancer's life. Above all, and it may seem obvious to state this, a dancer should love to dance.

Every day presents new challenges, new setbacks, and a subconscious feeling that all the effort and struggle may not be worth it in the end. Without sheer determination, a dancer is handicapped. The will to succeed in the face of adversity must be very strong indeed if the dancer is to overcome such inevitable feelings of frustration.

A dancer must be receptive. He or she must be quick to grasp new ideas and the impressions of others. Almost everything in ballet is a collaboration of one sort or other—collaboration between student and teacher, between partners, with the conductor, and especially with the choreographer. Choreography is, more often than not, a collaboration between creator and executor.

Patience is a virtue, especially in dance. Every little girl wants to be able to dance on point from her very first lesson, and I am certain that boys feel the same way about *double tours en l'air* and *grand jetés*. But these feats take years of training. Even the accomplished dancer will find some movements completely alien, and must work methodically and conscientiously to perfect them.

Most of a dancer's working life is spent in a classroom in front of a mirror. In this way dancers become aware of their own bodies and learn to make them move in the way they want. This brings an extraordinary satisfaction. The dancers come to know their own limitations and strengths.

A strong personality is a definite asset, for this projects across the footlights as readily and as surely as the most brilliant technique, and can conceal to a certain extent the physical limitations that every dancer has to one degree or another.

Technique, the basis of the art, is, of course, essential and is developed over years of training and hours and hours of bending, stretching, and extending various muscles. The artist with a virtuoso technique is truly blessed. In the end, however, it is how one uses that technique that separates the dancer from the athlete. Which brings us to the rather harder qualities to define—qualities such as grace, line, musicality, and dramatic ability.

Of these, grace and line are synonymous. A ballet is really a series of linked positions, gestures, and movements. Good line, as in sculpture, occurs when it seems that one could draw an unbroken line from the head, through the arms, upper body, down to the feet. It is easy to see how a jutting arm, a leg too highly extended, or a head placed too far forward in certain jumps can destroy the line, as well as the inherent grace. All movements in ballet must seem to flow harmoniously, and any awkward or jarring element shatters the effect.

Good line starts with a perfect turnout of the feet, a straight back, and proper placing of the head and arms. The dancer who is born with a well-proportioned body, with a slightly elongated neck, with beautiful arms and straight legs is at a distinct advantage compared to others less fortunate. Proper training and a critical eye can do much to improve line, while improper training can destroy it forever.

It would be wonderful if all dancers were musical —unfortunately, they are not. It is largely a matter of instinct. A child is either born with a love of or an ear for music or not. Parents can do much to instill a love of music in their children; it is axiomatic that a child who grows up listening to classical music will find it easier to relate to in later life. Learning to play an instrument like the piano is also beneficial, for a child is then actively participating in music. The child will understand something about what music is—that, like dancing, it is hard to perform well. Such a child will never again be passive in relation to music.

When creating a new ballet, the choreographer usually takes his inspiration from the music he has chosen, and so it should be with the dancer. A "musical" dancer is one who understands and feels the shape and the shadings of the score. One does not merely keep time with it; one relates to it. Naturally when learning a ballet, the dancer must be content for the moment with learning new steps and counting in time to make sure of entrances, exits, and placing. Then the dancer must listen harder to the score to learn the phrasing of it, rather like a singer. But once all of this is learned by rote and becomes automatic, the musical dancer listens, feels, and interprets. The music ceases merely to accompany; it dictates, it becomes the inspiration for every movement.

Dance is one of the performing arts, and a performing artist is, more often than not, an actor at heart. In many ways dance is drama distilled, because the whole range of human emotion must be expressed completely through the body. The dancer has no words to help. The function of ballet, or modern dance, is to tell a story or to express a point of view; to relay a mood or a feeling. It stands to reason that dramatic ability is very nearly as important to the dancer as the ability to negotiate difficult steps.

Some dancers are born with this natural dramatic ability. For others, it comes with experience. It follows that once one has performed a role several times, one can relax into it and concentrate more on its dra-

matic presentation; to some extent, the drama develops itself in the course of performances.

Throughout my life, I have always preferred the dramatic roles because I find the pure steps rather difficult and frightening. If I have a character to immerse myself in, I can think, for instance, about what Giselle is feeling and suffering and forget that the steps are difficult. If I am faced with a ballet that has no story at all and is really just a series of ballet steps, I am overconscious of the least fault in their execution and I find this inhibiting from the point of view of communicating dance to the public.

Finally, the most important quality a dancer can possess is also the one that is hardest to define. Talent for dancing is something that one is born with. Once it is discovered, it can be developed, it can be nurtured —but it can never ever be manufactured.

Curiously, although talent can be discerned in the

young, one can never be sure how far it will develop. There is also the question of physique, which complicates the issue. One looks first for the well-proportioned body, straight legs, suitable feet, and strong spine; with the ideal physique one can make an exceptional dancer—but one cannot add the "divine spark" of expression, emotion, or whatever it is that makes a rare artist.

On the other hand, the divine spark often turns up in a less than ideal physique. If it appears in a hopelessly proportioned body, there is nothing to be done, because the greatest violinist in the world cannot draw magic from an out-of-tune fiddle and the dancer's body is equivalent to his musical instrument. He depends upon it entirely to transmit his talent to the world.

Between the extremes of a perfect figure with no soul and a genius in the wrong-shaped body there are so many permutations that it is quite impossible to say what will make a good dancer and what will not. One must always remember that each one of us is an individual and cannot be ordered over the telephone like a Ford Mustang.

A BALLET COMPANY

Ballet is more than a profession—it is a way of life. A ballet company is simply a microcosm of that way of life. When a dancer is accepted, he or she joins an élite family of dedicated people all working toward the same goal with the same purpose. Companies vary considerably in size and scope, ranging from a handful of large and famous institutions like the Royal Ballet, American Ballet Theatre, and the New York City Ballet to smaller regional ones like the Scottish National Ballet and the Sacramento Civic Ballet.

Although it may be a dancer's dream to join a famous company, the importance of the smaller regional ones cannot be overstressed. These companies give dancers and choreographers the chance to develop at their own pace; they have the opportunity for experimentation without overexposure. Also, because of their smaller size, the dancer, especially at the beginning of a career, is given more work and more challenging roles than might be so if he or she had joined a larger company.

When I joined the Vic-Wells Company in 1933, there were only thirty-six dancers—perhaps only the director, Ninette de Valois, foresaw that it would grow into the Royal Ballet with a company nearing two hundred! Advancement is much slower now than in my time.

A dancer is accepted into a company in one of several ways. Very occasionally, a leading professional may be invited to join on the basis of exceptional talent. This is such a rare event that it is almost not worth mentioning. The two most common ways are either by audition or by graduating successfully from the school attached to the company—or attached to another important company.

This last method obviously has the most advantages. Ideally, all ballet companies should have their own schools, because students are trained from an early age to meet specific requirements. They grow up attending performances of the parent company, watching and learning from its dancers, so that by the time they graduate, even before they ever set foot on stage, they have a real idea and knowledge of the company's style and artistic demands.

Of course, attending this type of school does not automatically guarantee a place in the company. Students are watched very carefully, and are reassessed every year. Of the relatively few who complete their training successfully, a handful are invited to join the parent company; the rest are advised to attend auditions for other companies. It is a fact that students graduating from a school of this nature have a better than average chance of finding work. Tuition fees are invariably high, but there are government grants and scholarships available in certain circumstances.

When a student is finally accepted into a ballet company, there is an overwhelming sense of relief, of joy, and of accomplishment. At last he or she is a professional dancer, with a certain amount of emotional, artistic, and financial security.

All ballet companies are structured along similar

lines. Usually they are divided into three main categories: corps de ballet, soloists, and principals. The
fledgling dancer, except on rare occasions, starts his or
her professional life in the corps, the importance of
which cannot be overemphasized. Its function is to set
the mood of the ballet, to lend depth, continuity, and
presence to the whole. The emphasis here is most often
on precision and togetherness, and it is certainly true
that a well-trained and rehearsed corps can literally
make a company's reputation. Dancing in the corps,
the individual gains valuable stage experience. From
sheer repetition of movement, the brain is disciplined,
the body is strengthened, various difficulties are
worked out, and personality is developed. Of course,
the type of corps work varies from ballet to ballet
and from company to company. Some of it is extremely difficult, challenging, and hence rewarding
for the dancers; and occasionally it might be dull.

A soloist theoretically is no longer concerned with
corps work. He or she concentrates completely on solos,
pas de deux, and the occasional principal role. It is
with the soloist contract that the dancer begins to
dream of stardom and the final accolade, a principal
contract! That is the last moment at which anyone
should feel complacent. The higher a dancer rises in
the company, the greater is his or her responsibility
to justify expectations, and the critics do not always
appreciate what it means to hold the stage alone in
an important role for the first time.

The length of time spent in each of these particular categories is strictly dependent on the individual's
talent and ability. It is a sober fact of ballet life that
the majority of dancers never progress beyond the
corps. The world, fortunately, is made up of different people with different temperaments. Some are
ambitious, some are not. There must come a point in a

dancer's life where a certain amount of stocktaking is necessary. Some know they will never progress beyond the corps and face the fact with equanimity. They remain in the company because it has become their way of life and they are happy in the atmosphere of communal artistic enterprise—for one never really loses the sheer love of dancing. Some others ultimately decide it is not the life they truly want, and they find work in television, films, or the musical theatre— or they may leave the world of dance altogether for marriage and children or for another profession.

A typical day in a dancer's life begins with morning class. This usually lasts for an hour and a half, although on matinée days there may only be time for *barre* work without the center practice. This class is the most vital part of a dancer's life, a part that can never be ignored, because a dancer's body needs fine tuning to keep it in performing condition. The older a dancer becomes, the more important it is to take a daily class, for even after a week's holiday the muscles stiffen and do not respond.

In class, everyone from the corps to the principal dancer is subject to criticism and correction. After class, there are either full-company calls for various new ballets or more personal ones for dancers about to perform a role for the first time, or with different partners, and so on. New roles are the stuff of life for a dancer, and when such plums are landed it is a sure thing that every spare moment will be spent perfecting them.

"Lunch" (often just an apple and cheese and a yogurt) is usually taken in the staff canteen or at the café round the corner, and this is followed by more rehearsals, traditionally from 2 P.M. to 4 P.M., or perhaps by costume fittings. Also, most ballet companies have some kind of workshop whereby fledgling

dancer-choreographers can work with members of the company to present their new works on special evenings before an invited audience. In this way, even corps-de-ballet members get involved learning solo roles, and they are usually given afternoon rehearsal time. And it must be said that on an odd and blissful occasion, a dancer will have a completely free afternoon!

On performance evenings, everyone concerned must be at the theatre well in advance, because costume, make-up, and warming up take a good hour at least; personally, I always allow two hours. These activities can be quite therapeutic. Dancers are always keyed up before a performance. Some are more nervous than others, and the concentration involved in making up, for example, often has a calming effect.

For the next two and half hours, everything must go like clockwork. Dancers leave their real identities in the dressing room and become the characters they are portraying on the stage. The nerves that were present before seem to disappear on stage, because the dancer who is physically and mentally involved in the act of performing simply does not have the time to be nervous.

It is after the curtain comes down that a dancer's private life begins. It takes time to wind down after a performance, and although it is late, most dancers take this time to relax with friends over their main meal of the day—because few dancers like to eat much before the performance, although there are some who can sit down to a good steak and then go straight into the theatre for the show.

It is often said that ballet is a closed world, and in a way it is true. It is very difficult to make friends outside the company because of the hours involved in the dancer's job and the dedication required. It is difficult, but not impossible. A ballet dancer's life is certainly not easy and it might be prone to more disappointments than any other, yet the people who have chosen to pursue this way of life are for the most part happy, dedicated, and fulfilled, because they work continuously with a compatible group pursuing the same objectives and sharing their sorrows and triumphs.

TEACHERS' TRAINING

The first message of this book is that dancing is for everyone, or at least that it holds something for everyone who wants to involve himself in it, and that professional ballet is only a part of the whole, although it tends to catch most of the limelight.

The second message is that those wanting to study dance, and ballet in particular, should make every effort to be sure they have good teachers.

It may seem strange that in most countries there is no formal registration of dance teachers, and it is for this reason that various organizations—notably, England's Royal Academy of Dancing—have been established during the last fifty years or so to guide teachers on what to teach and how to go about it.

More recently, three-year training courses for dance teachers have been set up in one or two cities in England and Canada. Entry to these courses requires a certain level of practical accomplishment in ballet, and the curricula cover anatomy, principles of education, dance history, and various subjects equally important for young teachers in this age of unprecedentedly high standards at the corps-de-ballet level of all dance companies.

As more is expected of the corps-de-ballet dancers, it follows that more is expected of teachers at all levels,

especially for those who start young children on their
very first steps; so much depends on the initial placing of the body, and of the hip joints and the ankles
and feet. It is very necessary for teachers to compre-
hend clearly the mechanics of ballet technique and its
application to various shapes and sizes of human
form.

Graduates from the training courses are in immediate demand; often they have the opportunity to travel and take their first professional jobs with dancing academies far from their home countries. The prospects are good and the work interesting. More information can be found in the dance magazines.

DANCE AS A SUBJECT

Many students of dancing do not have the means or the physical structure to become professional dancers, and yet their intense love of the art seeks fulfillment in a career somehow involved with dance. If they have not taken any dance classes at all, it is difficult to take the subject at a high school or university, as a qualification for entry often involves some basic level of practical experience.

There are related studies that could lead to the world of dance; the first that comes to mind is stage management, which is of the greatest importance and can indeed make or mar a performance. Production has many departments, including scene painting, construction, the making of costumes and props. Perhaps the most difficult to achieve well is stage lighting, as it requires very special knowledge and imagination—also, I would say, a certain flair.

For the students who have taken dance to a particular elementary level, there are high school and college courses leading toward various basically amateur activities, as well as careers in dance history, writing and lecturing, notation, and anthropology. There are still areas of dance study that have been very little explored.

Dance as a Subject

In the United States, where there is an incredible surge of interest in dance, there is no exact parallel to the British educational certificates in dance, but it is possible to obtain a B.A. or even a master's degree in the subject as part of a university education. Dance departments are proliferating across the country.

CHOREOLOGY

A new career in the world of dance has opened up quite recently—that of choreologist, or dance notator. Choreology, defined as "the scientific and aesthetic study through notation of all forms of human movement," is a science that is still in its infancy. It has taken over five hundred years to perfect an orchestral score. It is fascinating to learn that although a successful system for writing down dance steps was published as early as the eighteenth century by a Frenchman, Raoul Feuillet, it was intended for social dance and therefore limited in its application. The perfected dance notation has only come into its own during the last fifty years.

There are two major notation systems in practice today. One is called Labanotation and was developed from a basis of Feuillet's work by the Hungarian Rudolf von Laban in 1928. The other was invented and copyrighted in 1955 by the English couple Rudolf and Joan Benesh and is called simply the Benesh system. One can study these two systems all over the world. Scores for various ballets are printed and can be bought and read like music.

Simply put, graduates of these two systems work extensively with the choreographer in the dance studio where a ballet or modern dance is created. As

BENESH

each movement is set, the choreologist writes it down, and when the work is completed, the notated score is kept as a permanent record. What was once confined to the choreographer's and dancers' memories is now recorded in minute detail in a manuscript, and can be sent anywhere in the world so it can be reproduced by other companies, just as music is at the fingertips of anyone who can read a score.

Labanotation is based on a three-line vertical staff, the center line representing the spine. It uses symbols and shadings to record the type and depth of movement, and has been used in America for many years. It is the system used to record many Broadway shows, as well as classical and modern works. Some Balanchine ballets have been Labanotated, as well as the works of modern dancers like Doris Humphrey and Martha Graham. When Humphrey's *The Shakers* was revived for the Welsh Dance Theatre in 1975, the

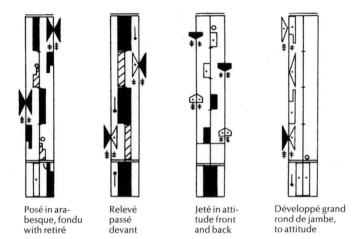

| Posé in ara-
besque, fondu
with retiré | Relevé
passé
devant | Jeté in atti-
tude front
and back | Développé grand
rond de jambe,
to attitude |

LABANOTATION

company used the Labanotation record of the original choreography.

The Benesh system is based on a five-line musical staff and is said to be easier to learn. It is a purely visual system, and the Royal Ballet uses it exclusively. The ballets of Ashton, MacMillan, de Valois, and Cranko are mounted all over the world with the aid of Benesh scores.

Naturally, in order to study and practice choreology, one has to have had a certain amount of professional dance training. It goes without saying that unless one has an extensive knowledge of the steps, it is impossible to write them down. The notation training is far from easy, requiring considerable patience and intelligence. It is, however, a fascinating and valuable study.

But the uses of choreology are not limited to dance. The medical profession has become increasingly interested in its application in conjunction with physiotherapy and with recording the movements of pre- and post-operative patients. Consequently, the Institute of Choreology in London has started giving introductory courses to registered physiotherapists.

Both forms of notation have also been used with a great deal of success in the field of dance anthropology—and what better way to study the nature of man than through his dances? For expressive movement is as old as time itself.

DANCE
AND ATHLETICS

Dancers are both athletes and artists, and increasingly gymnasts and other athletes find that dance classes are beneficial to their work. One has only to look at such sporting performers as John Curry, Olga Korbut, and Nadia Comaneci to understand what a great role modern dance and ballet play in their training.

A perfect example of this is John Curry. As a young boy, he wanted to become a dancer, but his father was against the idea and discouraged his son's interest in ballet. Consequently, Curry turned to ice skating, and his father voiced no objections because it was, after all, a sport. But as his training progressed, John realized that the kind of skating he was interested in had more to do with art and ballet technique than with conventional forms of athleticism. By then he was old enough to make up his own mind about ballet training, with or without parental approval. He found a sympathetic ballet teacher and started taking classes, which he continues today.

The performances that won him the British, World, and Olympic championship figure-skating titles in 1976 owed as much to ballet as they did to conventional ice-skating practice. Since then he has turned professional and has worked with ballet choreographers (including Kenneth MacMillan, Ronald Hynd, Peter Martins, and Jean-Pierre Bonnefous)

and with modern choreographers—Twyla Tharp, among others—to transpose dance choreography to the ice-skating stage. John Curry is a determined young man intent on developing ice skating as an art, and he is succeeding admirably.

In England and in the United States experiments have taken place involving soccer and football players with ballet classes. At the end of a chosen period, every football team, without exception, has had to acknowledge that the dancers' exercises were, both

physically and mentally, infinitely more demanding.

Ballet class has the power to extend considerably the original potential and mobility of any given set of muscles. Who knows what will ever stop man's progress in the realm of movement? For each year we see athletes and gymnasts setting astonishing new records and dance reaching out in exciting new directions. Dance and athletics thus share a seemingly limitless potential for pushing forward the frontiers of human endeavor.

FINALE

Voltaire said, "Dancing is an art because it has rules." And indeed the most effortless and natural-looking dance—which seems to have been improvised on the spot—must have its own system or technique. Without these foundations, the result is the kind of free expression—run around the room doing whatever you feel spontaneously—that was rather popular early in this century but actually did no one any good.

Self-expression is immensely important but can only be achieved through a set of rules. There are rules for putting letters together to make a word, for putting lines on a piece of paper to make a drawing, for putting color on canvas to make a painting, and for arranging notes of music to make a composition.

There is no way anything of value can be done without some framework. It might well be that the framework is discarded or the rules opposed; that is not important. What is essential is that they exist so that one knows when one is in opposition to them. It is not necessarily important that the rules be ideal or the framework perfect; not every system is right for every individual, so one cannot say categorically only this or that method is correct. One can usually say what is best within one field—for example, in classical ballet the correct technique is best because it gives the most fluent and the purest results, whereas exaggerations lead easily to acrobatic effects. Again, in acrobatics one notices at once the apparent lack of effort of the best technicians.

In whatever field of movement, the complete appearance or illusion of "freedom" is only achieved by maximum mastery of technique. The technique of modern dance is mostly unforced, following the body's natural movement dynamics, but it still has its own system. Whether it be the most difficult ballet step or the apparently most natural sway of the body, it can only be done well if it is studied and mastered. Some teachers concentrate so fixedly on the very difficult mechanics that the pupil ends up with astonishing virtuosity but no idea of how to enter or leave the stage. Who hasn't seen a dancer finish a brilliant solo and then bow to the public like a scarecrow in the wind and walk off like a duck?

Art is not confined to great art, but is just as much the art of doing simple things very well. Therefore it is always better to perform a minor role to perfection than to make a near miss of the principal part. The world of dance offers so many opportunities on different levels that there is a place for everyone who cares about it at all to participate. One can dance just for one's own enjoyment and satisfaction, or on stage for the enjoyment and satisfaction of others; or one can watch and appreciate; or one can study aspects of dance historically and anthropologically. It is a question of discovering the area in which the greatest fulfillment lies, and that is by no means always the obvious one in the limelight.

Fulfillment comes with the knowledge of having given one's whole concentration to the project at hand and having done it to the best of one's ability; that is the art of living. The magnitude of the job is not important, for it is as difficult (or more so) for an artist to paint a miniature as to paint a large canvas. In other words, quality is more important than quantity. Quality is art; unrestrained quantity is vulgarity. What Voltaire meant was simply that it is the rules that make the art.

APPENDIX

Ballet dancing in its present form is derived directly from the first professional school and ballet company, established in 1669 in Paris. The names of the steps are therefore all in French. Even in the seventeenth century they were not new but were terms used in the social dancing of the day. They described steps developed by the Italian and French dance teachers over a century and more; the origins of some steps lay in ethnic (or folk) dances. So even when professional ballet training was inaugurated, it employed timeworn steps.

With the passing of three hundred years, the usage of some movements has evolved considerably and so has the usage of the French language. Add to that the fact that French ballet terminology has been used worldwide, often by people with the scantiest knowledge of French, and you will understand why there are inconsistencies and confusions in its use and interpretation.

Without explaining the steps that bear these different French names, I am putting down in this appendix translations into English of some commonly used ballet terms. Italics indicate the interpretation closest to the term's application to dance.

ADAGIO (music) adagio, *slow* time
AIR air (*en l'air—in the air*)
ALLEGRO (music) *brisk* time
ALLONGÉ *lengthened, elongated*

APLOMB *equilibrium*, perpendicularity, *assurance*, self-command, self-possession

ARRIÈRE *behind* (*en arrière de—behind*)

ASSEMBLÉ *assembled*, united, joined

ATTITUDE *attitude*, posture, *pose*

AVANT *forward* (*en avant de—in front of*)

BALANCER to balance, to poise, *to swing*, to wave, *to rock*, to counterbalance

BALANÇOIRE *seesaw*

BALLON balloon, *India-rubber ball*

BALLONNÉ distended, swollen

BALLOTTÉ tossed, *tossed about*, kept in suspense, *bandied* (*a tennis ball*)

BARRE bar, rod *rail* (of metal, wood, etc.)

BAS *low*

BATTEMENT clapping (of hands), stamping (of feet), *flapping* (*of wings*), beating (of the heart), shuffling (of cards)

BATTERIE fight, scuffle, rough-and-tumble, *beat* (*of drum*), *roll* (*on side drum*), *quick succession of notes*

BATTU *beaten*, fought

BOURRÉE old French dance in three-quarter time

BRAS *arm* or *arms*

BRISÉ *broken*, folded

CABRIOLE *leap*, caper, goat's leap, somersault

CAMBRÉ *bent*, *arched*, well-set

CHANGEMENT *change*, alteration of course

CHASSÉ *chased*, pursued, hunted

CHAT *cat*

CHEVAL *horse*

CISEAUX *scissors*

CLOCHE *bell*

CONTRETEMPS note played, *step danced against the beat*, on the unaccented portion of the beat, out of time

CORPS body, *organized body* of men

CORYPHÉE coryphaeus, *leader of the chorus, leader of the ballet*

CÔTÉ *side* (*de côté—sideways*)

COU *neck*

COU-DE-PIED *instep*

COUPÉ *cut*, cut up, broken up, jerky style

COURONNÉ *crown, coronet*, wreath

COURU run, *running*

CROISÉ *crossed*

CROIX *cross* (*en croix—crosswise*)

CUISSE *thigh*

DE *of, for*, by

DÉBOULÉ *rolled* (*like a ball*)

DÉBUT *first appearance*, beginning

DEDANS within, *in*, inside (*en dedans—inward*)

DÉGAGÉ *disengaged*, redeemed, flippant, bold, easy

DEHORS *out*, without, outside (*en dehors—outward*)

DEMI *half*

DERRIÈRE *behind*

DESSOUS *under*

DESSUS *over*

DÉTOURNÉ *turned away*, retired, oblique

DEVANT *front*

DÉVELOPPÉ opened, unwrapped, *unfolded*, developed, expanded

DIVERTISSEMENT *diversion*, amusement, *entertainment*, recreation

DOS *back*, rear

DOUBLÉ *doubled*

DROITE *right* (*à droite—to the right*)

ÉCARTÉ set aside, removed, waived, passed over, dispelled, *widened*

ÉCHAPPÉ *escaped*, run away

EFFACÉ effaced, expunged, rubbed out, thrown into the shade (*s'effacer*—to draw aside, *to give way, to turn the body sideways*)

ÉLANCÉ launched, *darted*, shot

EMBOÎTÉ jointed, set, *fitted, fitted in*

EN *in*, into, within, on, *to, at, like*

ENCHAÎNEMENT chain, *series, logical sequence*

ENCHAÎNER to chain up, enchain, *to link*

ENTRECHAT caper, cross caper

ENTRÉE *entrance, entry, entering, coming in*, reception, beginning, introduction

ENTRELACÉ intertwined, interlaced, interwoven

ENVELOPPÉ *enveloped, wrapped up*, covered, folded up

ÉPAULÉ *push (with the shoulder)*, shouldering

ÉPAULEMENT a shoulder piece, *shoulder*

ÉQUILIBRE *balance, equilibrium, poise*

ÉTOILE *star*

FACE *front (de face de*—in front of, *full face*) (*en face de*—in the face of, opposite)

FAILLI *missed*, failed, trespassed, transgressed, mistaken

FERMÉ *closed*, shut

FLÈCHE *arrow*, dart, shaft

FONDU *melted*, dissolved, *softened* (fondue—melted cheese)

FOUETTÉ *whipped*, streaked (flowers), whipped (cream)

FRAPPÉ *struck*, smitten, slapped, tapped, *hit*

GARGOUILLADE a rattling, a rumbling, a dabbling, *a paddling*

GAUCHE *left (à gauche*—to the left)

GLISSADE *sliding*, slide, slipping, slip

GLISSÉ *slide, glide*

GRAND great, large, *high*, lofty, tall, wide, *big*, huge, grand

HAUT *high*, tall (*en haut*—upstairs)

JAMBE *leg*, shank

JETÉ *thrown*, cast

LEVÉ *lifted, raised up*

LIÉ bound, *tied*, friendly, intimate

MAILLOT *tights*, jersey

MAÎTRE *master* (*maître à danser—dancing master, maître de ballet—ballet master*)

MANÈGE horsemanship, *riding school*

MARCHE *walk, walking*, advance, step

OUVERT *open*

PAS *step*, pace, footstep (*pas de—step of*) (*pas seul—solo; pas de deux—dance for two; pas de trois—dance for three, etc.; pas de basque—Basque step, etc.*)

PASSÉ *passed*

PENCHÉ bent, *leaning*

PETIT *small, little*, diminutive, short

PIED *foot*

PIQUÉ *pricked*, stung

PIROUETTE *rapid whirling round*, whirligig

PLIÉ *folded* (*bend of knee in dancing*)

POINTE *point* (*sur les pointes—on the toes*)

POINTÉ *pointed*

POINTU *pointed, sharp, peaked*

POISSON *fish*

PORT harbor, port, *carriage* (of parcels), presence, *bearing*, gait (*port de bras—carriage of the arms*)

PORTÉ *carried*, inclined, prone, disposed

POSE *posture, attitude*

POSÉ *poised*, bearing, resting, leaning

POSER *to place*, to set, to lay down

RACCOURCI *shortened*, abbreviated

RAMASSÉ *gathered up*, compact, clustered

RELEVÉ *raised*, erect, high, exalted, refined

RENVERSÉ *reversed, turned upside down*

RÉPÉTER to repeat

RÉPÉTITION repetition, *rehearsal*

RETIRÉ retired, *withdrawn, contracted*, secluded

RÉVÉRENCE reverence, *bow, curtsy*

ROND *round,* ring, *circle,* disk

SAUT *leap, jump,* skip, bound

SAUTÉ *jumped*

SCÈNE *scene,* stage

SERRÉ *close,* compact, tight

SOUBRESAUT sudden start, bound, leap (of horse, etc.)

SOUTENU *sustained,* unremitting, unceasing, unfailing

TEMPS *measure* (of music), beat, stress, accent

TENDU stretched, strained, tense, taut, tight

TERRE earth, land, *ground,* territory (*à terre—on the ground*)

TOMBÉ *fallen,* fallen down, *dropped down*

TOUR rotation, *turn*

TOURNANT *turning*

VOLÉ stolen, robbed, *taken away, flown, soared*

NUMBERS

UN, UNE	one	SEPT	seven
DEUX	two	HUIT	eight
TROIS	three	NEUF	nine
QUATRE	four	DIX	ten
CINQ	five	ONZE	eleven
SIX	six	DOUZE	twelve

POSITIONS

PREMIÈRE first

DEUXIÈME (SECONDE) second

TROISIÈME third

QUATRIÈME fourth

CINQUIÈME fifth

ILLUSTRATIONS
AND CREDITS

The author and the publisher would like to
thank the following individuals and collections
by whose kind permission the illustrations
are reproduced.

Illustrations and Credits

A NOTE ON THE TYPE

THE TEXT OF THIS BOOK was set in Waverley, a typeface produced by the Intertype Corporation. Named for Captain Edward Waverley, the hero of Sir Walter Scott's first novel, it was inspired by the spirit of Scott's literary creation rather than actually derived from the typography of that period. Indeed, Waverley is a wholly modern typeface, if not by definition, certainly by association with the designs of the best contemporary typographers.

The book was composed by American Book–Stratford Press, Inc., Brattleboro, Vermont; it was printed and bound by Halliday Lithograph, West Hanover, Massachusetts.

Rochambeau Branch